The Beginner's Guide to Traveling in the Spirit

Written by Michael C. King

This book and other titles by Michael King can be found at TheKingsofEden.com

Available from Amazon.com, Createspace.com, and other retail outlets.

ISBN-13: 978-1-946252-02-9
ISBN-10: 1946252026

Table of Contents

Dedication

I dedicate this book to the forerunners—to those hungry seekers who push at the boundaries of "normal" and won't settle for anything less than everything God has planned for them. You have pushed ahead and broken ground when criticism was coming from all directions. You have stood tall in the face of opposition when no one was standing behind you in support. You are overcomers who are even now making a path for others to follow, and creating a platform so others can join you. Thank you for your tireless efforts to reveal God's truth and love to the world.

But on you will go though the weather be foul. On you will go though your enemies prowl. On you will go though the Hakken-Kraks howl. Onward up many a frightening creek, though your arms may get sore and your sneakers may leak. On and on you will hike. And I know you'll hike far and face up to your problems whatever they are.

- Dr. Seuss in *Oh The Places You'll Go* -

Acknowledgements

Thank you to my wife Sunshine for providing the idea to write this book and for your ever-amazing editing work, and to Mahesh Taank for providing the confirmation from God to go ahead and write it. Thank you to Ben Valence for being that person I could talk to and confide in when spirit travel was still a taboo subject. Thank you to Dave and Denise Hayes for helping me through some rough spots, as well as to Denise Hayes studios for your stellar-as-always design work. A special thanks to my dear friend Hope for providing such deeply moving testimonies for this book—I trust they will minister to many as much as they have touched me.

Preface

Back in 2006, when the subject of Spirit Travel was kept severely under wraps and no *Bible*-based teaching existed on the subject, I was in a ministry school in Harrisburg, PA. As part of our coursework, the students took turns preaching to the group for practice, with the entire class cycling twice each year. For my first message I had prepared a teaching about seeing in the spirit from the book of Ezekiel, but about two weeks before I spoke someone else shared a very similar message, so I scrapped it and went back to the drawing board. One night, while I was praying in the living room of my dorm apartment, I saw in the spirit a rectangular golden door open before me and an angel step through it. He turned, rolled the doorway up from bottom to top as though it were a scroll, then turned and shoved it into my chest. I began to read various Scriptures, and received much revelation at that time.

Out of that experience, the Lord gave me a message about spiritual gatekeepers and the keys to the Kingdom, which I preached on that following week. These gatekeepers have been assigned the task of opening the heavens for others. Interestingly, in Matthew 23:13 Jesus got angry with the spiritual leaders of his day for their failures as gatekeepers: "Woe to you, teachers of the law and Pharisees, you hypocrites! You shut the door of the kingdom of heaven in people's faces. You yourselves do not enter, nor will you let those enter who are trying to." He noted that the Pharisees and other teachers truly *did* have the ability to open and close the heavens for others, and his indictment was their failure to both make access open for others and for their *failure to use it themselves.*

I did not realize it at the time, but that message, explaining how God has called and positioned people to open access to the heavenly realms, has described a good portion of what God has done in my life since—paving the way to bring others into deeper spiritual life and experiences than they have had before. Additionally, the Lord began to regularly reveal portals to me—doorways in the spirit by which angels, demons, and other spiritual beings traverse the spiritual spheres.

Spirit travel is important to me because I believe it is a gateway to deeper realms of spiritual life. This is the tenth year since that time, and the Lord has consistently reminded me that He is renewing and returning me to many of those things He did in my life back then. It feels quite fitting that during this anniversary-year I am publishing a book to do exactly what He showed me during that angelic encounter—open up access to the spiritual realms. It is my sincere desire that this book helps launch you into deeper encounters with the Living God as you travel through the heavens and the earth in this *Beginner's Guide to Traveling in the Spirit.*

-Michael C. King-

Chapter 1

How It All Began

Spirit Travel has gradually become familiar to me since I first tried it in 2005, a good year and a half before I entered that ministry school. I was in a period of intensified spiritual growth and spent a lot of time practicing and engaging the prophetic. On rare occasion, I had visions that felt much more real than I could otherwise explain—as if I was just a thread away from actually tasting, hearing, and smelling the things I encountered. One of these was during a Wednesday night church membership class. My good friend and mentor Diane led this particular class, part of a lengthy curriculum that covered the theological basics according to that church. I don't recall when or why it happened, but we were on the second floor of the education building and I had a vision of a dark stone room. Light shone through a doorway across the room, but the room itself was in shadows. I could see a raised circular platform in the middle of this chamber with what looked almost like a large stone vase or chalice in the middle. I stepped up to it and found it filled to the brim—making the whole device much like an ornate baptismal font or a fountain. It was similar to what one might imagine The Mirror of Galadriel from the Lord of the Rings to be like.

This vision felt more *real* than normal to begin with, but as I looked into the water, a scene began to form in its depths. Three horses with riders on their backs charged across a desert, and I could literally feel myself *pulled* somehow into this scene. I heard the shriek of a bird of prey as well. It was odd because I was acutely aware of the class being taught around me but I was trying to ignore it to focus on this unexpected vision, and the sounds that were so real in my spirit that I felt I could *almost* hear them with my physical ears. The sensation I felt was as though something was getting sucked out of my body to dive deeper into the waters and enter the desert.

As this was happening I didn't understand what was going on except that I assumed God was advancing me in the prophetic— moving me from having visions to prophetic *experiences*. Eventually, I lost my focus and shifted my attention back to the class, the suction feeling fading, visionary experience over—but thirteen years later that event obviously stuck with me as I have not, to my recollection, ever written it down prior to now. I didn't realize it at the time, but I believe that was the first time I ever was consciously involved in spirit travel. From that point on, God began drawing me deeper into things prophetic, which would eventually be played out when I took my first intentional trip to the heavens.

During that phase of my life, God invariably dropped little hints my way about things. When I listened to preaching messages, the strange things usually stuck with me. This still happens to this day, and it seems to me a little bit like playing a game of connect the dots, or how people draw constellations out of the stars. One isolated item doesn't mean anything, but when strung together with a series of other data points, a bigger picture emerges. Traveling in the spirit was like this for me.

I remember a message minister Todd Bentley preached where he quoted Ephesians 2:6 saying, "And God raised us up with Christ and seated us with him in the heavenly realms in Christ Jesus." Todd shared that he believed an experience goes along with that statement people usually read as positional theology, and if there was an experience to have, he wanted to have it. I heard another message by Patricia King, minister and founder of Extreme Prophetic, where she told a story. In her story, she, Bob Jones, and someone else were meeting together. Bob took their hands and simply said, "Ascend," and up they went in the spirit! I am certain that I heard these messages months apart from one another, but those factoids stuck with me, revealing that something deeper was available. Another time Todd Bentley shared how he was ascending in the spirit and was stopped by a demonic entity, but ignoring the detail that he never completed his journey, the fact remains he was indeed traveling in the spirit. Here I was wanting to learn how to prophesy better and see angels (and I still want all of that even though I am more experienced now than I was then), but these people were talking about taking trips to heaven, and they made it sound like this was entirely normal!

David Hogan, founder of Freedom Ministries and a minister to the natives in Mexico and other parts of North and South America, preached a message many years ago where he spoke about how one of his pastors was killed by a principality that walked into this man's hut in the form of a four-foot hoot-owl. David shared that this man's spirit was dragged from his body to a gathering of local black-magic warlocks. This pastor's wife prayed and he was resurrected, his spirit returned to his body, but not before his spirit-man had already seen the identities of these warlocks—men and women who had been living among them and keeping their satanic practices secret.

All of these stories only served to further cement inside me that spirit travel was not only possible but that it was something God designed for us to experience. After all, why talk about it in the *Bible* as a scriptural promise if it is unavailable to us as believers? I have a habit of pondering these sorts of things, gleaning insights and uncovering deeper spiritual truths within them as I do. And with these seemingly unrelated messages, I realized that there were these different *Bible* verses that all suggested a higher spiritual experience than I was having, and like Todd Bentley, if there is a Godly spiritual experience available, I want it.

Ephesians 1:3 says, "Praise be to the God and Father of our Lord Jesus Christ, who has blessed us in the heavenly realms with every spiritual blessing in Christ." These spiritual blessings are from God to us, but the way we access them is *in the heavenly realms*—so if I want to receive these blessings I might need to head to the heavens to get them! Ephesians 2:6 says that, "And God raised us up with Christ and seated us with him in the heavenly realms in Christ Jesus . . ." I don't know about you, but if we are seated with Jesus in the heavenly realms, then I'd very much like to have the experience of being seated to go along with the theoretical seating that I already am now in Christ. Colossians 3:1 says, "If then you have been raised with Christ, seek the things that are above, where Christ is, seated at the right hand of God." This verse directly tells us to seek spiritual things and to do so by going to where Jesus is seated in the throne room right next to the Father. Hebrews 4:16 tells us to "approach God's throne of grace with confidence, so that we may receive mercy and find grace to help us in our time of need." If we are to appear before God's throne, then we have to actually be *in* His throne room, which is located in heaven, and the *Bible* tells us to do it with boldness!

After a while of pondering these verses, along with the stories these preachers and prophetic teachers were sharing, I couldn't help but sense something more—something I was missing. As I considered these things, I started to wonder how I could choose to go into the heavens. If Bob Jones could grab peoples' hands and say the word "ascend" and up they go, it meant this is possible, but *how* did he do it? How did he take people *with* him? And how can I have this same experience of being in heavenly places like the Scriptures say I am?

This led me on a covert journey. I assumed that if I told anyone what I was thinking they would have flipped their lids, and as time went on I realized I suspected rightly. I knew I was exploring new territory, but I didn't have anyone who I trusted would help me do so, which was disappointing. This left me with a fear that I could get led astray in some yet-unknown manner, but I had an equally strong conviction that there was something out there still to be had. Thus, I pursued this line of reasoning, but did so cautiously, prayerfully, silently, and slowly.

Eventually, God brought me an opportunity in the form of a guy around my age, named Ben, whom I had befriended the year prior at a conference. Occasionally, we chatted on the phone and discussed all sorts of spiritual things, especially about healing and the prophetic—visions, dreams, discernment of spirits, and more.

The first time I ever tried to purposefully ascend into the heavens, I was driving alone in my car on a two-hour car trip to visit that ministry school I later attended. I had called Ben to chat on the ride, and our conversation quickly shifted to the idea of accessing the heavenly realms freely. Up until that point, I was the only person I knew who believed that was possible. It turned out that Ben was experiencing the very things I had been pondering. It was validating, and I was relieved I had someone to share my secret with. Furthermore, it encouraged me that I was on the right path.

Ben told me about the first time he went to heaven in the spirit. A seer-prophet friend of his verbally walked Ben through what he would experience based on his own previous encounter. At first Ben began imagining the things this seer was telling him, as if going through guided imagery. If his friend said there was a tree to his right, Ben would imagine that. Then he started to step out in faith to see what else he could visualize. Ben began to engage this visionary experience, and somewhere along the line it stopped being just imagination and transitioned into him interacting in the actual place in heaven his friend was describing. All of this took place inside his mind, displayed on the backdrop of his imagination in the same way we experience visions and dreams.

Right there on the phone he began telling me about it and what everything looked like so that I could try it myself later, cautioning me to try when I was not driving. The thing is that I am a visual person to begin with, so while he was describing it, I naturally envisioned it in my head, almost the same as if I was having a vision. Partway through his guided tour of this place in heaven, I realized I was actually doing it right then, on the phone, while driving on the highway.

I have been back to that place multiple times since then, and one time I ended up on a horse that took me to a city where I had an encounter with Jesus that brought me some inner healing. Any time I return to a location I have been, the process is much like how it was when Ben guided me that first time. I begin remembering and imagining what it was like the previous occasion, with the intent that I'm going to actually *be* there. As I do that, I begin to experience it in my mind on the backdrop of my imagination once more. We have this belief in religious circles that spiritual things must be hard to attain and are acquired through effort and constant practice. While it is true that we develop abilities through practice over time, Jesus said that his yoke is easy and his burden is light. Spirit travel is meant to be as well. It can be difficult to wrap our minds around the idea that we can experience heavenly realities in our mind's eye while still interacting with the material world around us, but experience has shown me that we can legitimately experience heaven in this way.

One of the things I discovered after beginning my hush-hush journey delving into spirit travel was that a select few leaders in the Body of Christ were beginning to speak out about this publically. Actually, outside of the few stories I have shared in this chapter of tidbits in certain speakers' messages, there was only one man, Bruce Allen of Still Waters International Ministries, who I ever heard speak on the subject as early as 2007, years after the Lord introduced me to this topic. I am thankful for his tenacity in pursuit of all that God has for us, because I recognize that over the years he must have endured much ridicule from the Church for taking the stance that he has. The good news is that now, a decade later, things have both changed and continue to rapidly change in the Body of Christ in this area.

On May 7, 2012 I posted a blog on social media titled *To Project or Not to Project: That IS The Question*. It was quite controversial at the time, but I posted it based on a principle I prefer to live by: Regarding what are typically known as taboo subjects, I believe if no one is ever willing to step out and discuss them, becoming the first to take the hits from the rest of the Body, no one else will be willing to come out of the crowd either. In other words, it takes someone to pioneer a matter to make room for early adopters. In the Church we call these people *forerunners*. As the early adopters come on board, it makes room for the majority to eventually follow suit. I got a lot of negative feedback for that message, getting kicked out of a prophetic group I helped establish and administrate, had a stream of accusations flying around behind my back, and things as a whole blew up in this area. In fact, I only knew about some of this because the perpetrators had secret conversations with some of my closest friends about it, who then notified me. All this because I had the audacity to think original thoughts and share them with others.

As a side note, we need to understand this is why many people are unwilling to take risks and speak up about their experiences—because when someone like me steps out and does so, the persecution comes from all sides. Most people are unwilling to purposefully paint targets on their backs, and as a result we all miss out.

The good news is that in spite of the early friction, this note was eventually well-received by many, sparking other, later conversations on this subject. Among the spheres of influence that some of my fellow authors and I have, we were able to successfully steer not only the conversation toward open learning and discussion, but I believe that our candidness in exploring spirit travel has helped entire groups of people feel safe when it came time to hear more well-known speakers who have since come onto the scene. Only five years ago this subject was still almost entirely taboo, yet after a shift in language and understanding, in 2017, people are even hosting conferences and preaching entire message series surrounding this subject of spirit travel. While maturity is still needed in this area, the Body of Christ is rapidly taking ground and I believe that things will only get better from here.

Chapter 2

The Biblical Value of Spirit Travel

One of the first things people ask when discussing the validity of traveling in the spirit is the purpose—what is the point? This is a key question because until we understand why we want to do it, spirit travel can seem irrelevant or a sidetrack somehow regarding the purposes of the Gospel. Right alongside that question is, "Where is spirit travel in the *Bible*?" Rest assured it *is* in the Scriptures, and we will take a look. In this chapter I will address why spirit travel is valuable and important, and then look at the various places it is found in Scripture, in both the Old and New Testaments.

Why Spirit Travel?

Contrary to what some believe, spirit travel has many uses and can be a highly functional part of Christian ministry. With it we can combat forces of darkness, heal the sick and perform other forms of supernatural ministry, as well as obtain heavenly revelation. I am certain other applications exist as well, but these appear to be the most common.

I recall hearing Ian Clayton, a well-known speaker who now discusses the subject of spirit travel somewhat regularly, publically share the following story. While traveling and ministering, he decided to check in on one of his businesses to see how things were going. He went there in the spirit and witnessed an employee taking money from the till. He dialed up the store and spoke to her about it, informing her that he knew she was stealing and that he expected her to return the money. Not only was she shocked to hear his call, but he had seen correctly—she was indeed stealing from his business.

Spirit travel is not meant to simply be a spying-tool, although it can be used as such. The United States Government actually spearheaded the StarGate Project back in the 1970s, which has since become public record. The goal was to use supernatural abilities to collect intelligence on enemy activities while seeing in the spirit from afar—hence the reason it became known as Remote Viewing. The message the government gave the public is that the program was a failure, later declassifying operation documents, but the ability to Remote View itself is not. Whether for personal or governmental use, it is possible to gather information by spirit travel. I have done so on more than one occasion, although I prefer to use it either when practicing, which I do infrequently, or when checking on someone I am concerned about, which I do even more rarely. Once I was unable to get a hold of a friend in a problematic situation, but by viewing her in the spirit I was able to see she was indeed safe which allayed my concerns.

Combat Forces of Darkness

When we travel in the spirit we have the ability to more directly and visibly address demonic activity, engaging the enemy in heavenly combat. I elaborate further on this subject in Chapter 10. In addition to the fact that simply engaging our spiritual senses helps us to become aware of such activity, as we go through the heavens, we can actively thwart plans of the enemy. Certainly normal methods of intercession can accomplish this, but battling more actively into the heavens can provide an increased measure of effectiveness when fighting against powers of darkness. After all, Ephesians 6:12 reminds us, "For our struggle is not against flesh and blood, but against the rulers, against the authorities, against the powers of this dark world and against the spiritual forces of evil *in the heavenly realms* (*emphasis mine*)." This battle we wage is spiritual, and when a spiritual battle occurs in the heavens, it seems only sensible that we should engage it there.

One key component of earthly warfare is that it is always better to fight on someone else's territory than it is to do so on our own. While someone else's territory is unfamiliar, to do it on our own soil means we have already been invaded, and it is far better to prevent invasion than it is to have to fight off an incursion when it comes to home soil. Instead of waiting until we have problems that manifest in the material realm, we can fight spiritual forces of wickedness in the heavens.

Supernatural Ministry

One of the benefits of traveling in the spirit is the ability to heal the sick from afar. This is not the only kind of supernatural ministry that is possible, but it is one of the more notable. Once, years ago, I chanced across a story of an elderly gentleman who was bedbound. He was heartsick because he had recently come to know Jesus and didn't have the ability to share the gospel with anyone. He pleaded with the Lord to give him an opportunity to speak the good news of Jesus Christ with someone, so on one occasion he was taken in a trance and appeared before the bedside of a sick individual in a hospital. He was able to pray with this person and explain the gospel to him or her, and afterwards was transported back to his bed. While it might sound at first like he was moved bodily, it seems much more likely given his inability to move around physically that his spirit went to minister to that person instead.

Other saints throughout history have been known to do such things. Possibly the most well-known is Padre Pio, who is purported to have bilocated multiple times.

> Among the most remarkable of the documented cases of bilocation was the Padre's appearance in the air over San Giovanni Rotondo during World War II. While southern Italy remained in Nazi hands American bombers were given the job of attacking the city of San Giovanni Rotondo. However, when they appeared over the city and prepared to unload their munitions a brown-robed friar appeared before their aircraft. All attempts to release the bombs failed. In this way Padre Pio kept his promise to the citizens that their town would be spared. Later on, when an American airbase was established at Foggia a few miles away, one of the pilots of this incident visited the friary and found to his surprise the little friar he had seen in the air that day over San Giovanni. As to how Padre Pio with God's help accomplished such feats, the closest he ever came to an explanation of bilocation was to say that it occurred "by an extension of his personality" (Padre).

Ministering to people in the spirit is something that can be done at any time. I often do it when praying for people from a distance, especially when someone needs healing. Sometimes, praying for someone in this manner yields useful information about contributing factors to their malady. When I engage the matter spiritually, I can often identify spiritual realities such as demons and other negative energies that are often attributed to emotional issues. This allows me to either work through those hindrances or notify the person of my observations, providing them with the revelation they need to take their healing a step further.

I have heard stories of people actually being able to feel a presence in the room or sense physical touch when someone's spirit is laying hands on them. Think about how revolutionary this can be! We know conceptually that our prayers are not limited by time or space, but experientially we are finding this to be true more and more as we spirit travel. Whether the need is healing for a physical malady or something else entirely, this method of travel has limitless potential to touch lives.

This phenomenon is not limited to ministering to other people. Spirit travel allows us to go beyond our normal human limitations and influence the natural realm in a deeper way—altering weather patterns, shifting tectonic plates, and more. One of the reasons for this is that as we travel we engage the spiritual beings who are involved with those celestial and earthly movements. As we take dominion over the spirits who are ruling over the earth, wind, and waves, we will find in the days subsequent to our spiritual encounters that even news reports will corroborate the things we have seen and done in the spiritual atmospheres of the earth.

Heavenly Revelation

One of the benefits of spirit travel is receiving revelation from Heaven. I have had a number of spiritual encounters involving travel into the heavens that have brought new revelation. When we experience heavenly realities, the options open wide before us—to the point that some of us have held conversations with saints of old through these spiritual encounters. I have heard a few people share testimonies of having spoken with Enoch, and I have on a few different occasions had conversations with Jesus or other Biblical figures. If we understand that we are surrounded by a great cloud of witnesses (Hebrews 12:1), it is not unreasonable to think that in our spiritual travels we might bump into them from time to time.

In the book *The Final Quest*, Rick Joyner shares an encounter he had where he found himself in the throne room in heaven, and as he walked toward the throne he had a number of different conversations with men and women who have died and are now in heaven. Some of them were people he knew personally and not just historically. The conversations he shared in that book, ones he had when speaking with men and women beyond the veil, are indeed revelatory, share unique insights into aspects of his spiritual walk, and I suggest are equally relevant to ours as well. Spirit travel is by no means the only preferred method of gaining heavenly revelation, but it is an option we should be aware of, and it is something we can add to the proverbial tool belt.

Where is it in the *Bible*?

Now that we have looked at some of the ways traveling in the spirit can be utilized, where do we see this in the *Bible*? How do we know this is not just some occult power that God doesn't want us to touch? There are a number of verses, both in the Old and New Testaments that either directly speak of spiritual travel in some manner or allude to concepts that are contained therein.

One of the most obvious, and first-appearing, involved the prophet Elisha and his servant Gehazi. 2 Kings 5:24-26 says:

When Gehazi came to the hill, he took the things from the servants and put them away in the house. He sent the men away and they left.

When he went in and stood before his master, Elisha asked him, "Where have you been, Gehazi?"

"Your servant didn't go anywhere," Gehazi answered.

But Elisha said to him, "Was not *my spirit with you* when the man got down from his chariot to meet you? Is this the time to take money or to accept clothes—or olive groves and vineyards, or flocks and herds, or male and female slaves *(emphasis mine)*?

If we look at the master-apprentice relationship Elijah set up with Elisha, it is likely that Gehazi had the same relationship with Elisha, and presumably would have inherited the prophetic mantle—if he had made different choices along the way. This incident was the turning point in that relationship. Elisha clearly stated that *his spirit* was with Gehazi. It shows us that not only did the prophet possess the ability to do this at will, but that Elisha did this regularly to check in on his servant's activities.

Elisha apparently made frequent use of this ability because during wartime he would tell the King of Israel the enemy armies' plans. While the passage that shares this story, 2 Kings 6:8-12, doesn't explicitly state that the prophet was spiritually spying, it is highly suggestive that he was doing so. The King of Aram called his officers in after a foiled plot, asking who the mole was. One of the officers responded in verse 12 saying, "None of us, my lord the king . . . but Elisha, the prophet who is in Israel, tells the king of Israel the very words you speak in your bedroom." While the prophet could simply have gotten words of knowledge about things, the idea that Elisha would hear conversations the King of Aram held in his private chambers is suggestive of more than just getting divine downloads. It seems more likely he was directly spiritually spying on the enemy. I know how the prophetic works, and while God can and does warn people of impending trouble, we have the ability to direct some of the revelation we receive. In keeping with the previous passage about Gehazi, we already know Elisha had the ability to spirit travel, so it seems reasonable he would have done the same here, to the point that enemy officers included that fact in their intelligence report to the King.

Yet again in the Old Testament, Ezekiel 37 speaks of an encounter the prophet Ezekiel had where Holy Spirit picked him up and set him in a valley in the midst of dry bones with an instruction to prophesy and decree life to them. While the passage could be read as either being physically translocated or taken to a location in the spirit realm, either is possible and the passage doesn't preclude the possibility of having traveled to a spiritual dimension. I share a story in the last chapter of my book *Feathers From Heaven* where a man was taken in trance into a spiritual encounter to Ezekiel's valley of dry bones. He picked something up and placed it in his pocket while in the valley of bones, and upon coming out of the trance he found a large, fluffy, beautiful white feather in that pocket. Spirit travel is very real and can be very powerful.

Spirit Travel occurred in the New Testament as well—I suggest Jesus has done it. John 1:47-48 says:

> When Jesus saw Nathanael approaching, he said of him, "Here truly is an Israelite in whom there is no deceit."
>
> "How do you know me?" Nathanael asked.
>
> Jesus answered, "I saw you while you were still under the fig tree before Philip called you.

Jesus didn't specify that he had a vision of Nathanael—he stated he saw him. In fact, the Greek word there is *eido* which means to see or perceive with the eyes (Strong). It can also mean to know information or knowledge, but even under the circumstances that it was via spiritual perception only, the information still came through spiritual sight. The possibility that Jesus traveled in the spirit and observed Nathanael in-person cannot be ruled out.

In fact, Jesus actually had a habit of doing that sort of thing. In Mark 6:45-48 he was on the side of a mountain and somehow managed to see his disciples struggling out in the middle of a massive lake. Unless he had supernatural eagle-eyes, he was checking up on them in the spirit, which is the more likely option of the two.

The apostle Paul was known for his ability to travel in the spirit, to the point that he shared this fact freely in his letters to the churches. 1 Corinthians 5:3 says, "For my part, even though I am not physically present, *I am with you in spirit.* As one who is present with you in this way, I have already passed judgment in the name of our Lord Jesus on the one who has been doing this *(emphasis mine)*." Again in Colossians 2:5 he said to the church in Colossae, "For though I am absent from you in body, *I am present with you in spirit* and delight to see how disciplined you are and how firm your faith in Christ is *(emphasis mine)*." Paul clearly states that while not there in person, he is there *in spirit.* How much clearer could that be, especially when he said it not once but twice—to two different churches?

Paul had another encounter early on post-conversion that he shared with the Corinthian church. This experience is a little less clear due to the nature of the event, but it certainly leaves room for the possibility that the Apostle was spirit traveling at the time. In 2 Corinthians 12:2-4 Paul wrote:

> I know a man in Christ who fourteen years ago was caught up to the third heaven. Whether it was in the body or out of the body I do not know—God knows. And I know that this man—whether in the body or apart from the body I do not know, but God knows—was caught up to paradise and heard inexpressible things, things that no one is permitted to tell.

He was so engrossed in this spiritual experience that it was impossible for him to tell just how involved he was—whether it was in spirit only or if his body was caught up into the heavens as well.

Jesus and Paul were not the only ones in the New Testament who traveled in the spirit. John the Revelator did as well—to the point that the majority of the book of Revelation is the result of a series of encounters he had while in the spirit. Revelation 1:9-10 states:

> I, John, your brother and companion in the suffering and kingdom and patient endurance that are ours in Jesus, was on the island of Patmos because of the word of God and the testimony of Jesus. On the Lord's Day I was *in the Spirit*, and I heard behind me a loud voice like a trumpet . . . *(emphasis mine)*.

The rest of the book of Revelation continues from there, with angelic encounters, visions, and more—all of which occurred while he was *in the spirit*.

There is additional scriptural evidence that suggests we are expected to engage the spiritual realms in a more purposeful manner. Ephesians 1:3 says, "Praise be to the God and Father of our Lord Jesus Christ, who has blessed us in the heavenly realms with every spiritual blessing in Christ." Ephesians 2:6-7 states, "And God raised us up with Christ and seated us with him in the heavenly realms in Christ Jesus, in order that in the coming ages he might show the incomparable riches of his grace, expressed in his kindness to us in Christ Jesus." Both of these verses state clearly that we are *in the heavenly realms* and even that we obtain blessings when we are found in the heavens. Colossians 3:1 says, "If then you have been raised with Christ, seek the things that are above, where Christ is, seated at the right hand of God." We are encouraged to actively *seek things above*, and if that wasn't clear enough, Paul clarified where "above" is—in the throne room of Heaven.

Traveling in the spirit is a very Biblical practice. Furthermore, its functionality does not end with the canon of Scripture, but continues on into the present day. If we can see evidence of this practice in the Old Testament by multiple prophets, in both the Gospels and Epistles of the New Testament, and in the book of Revelation, it stands to reason that this is a spiritual reality God has designed and apportioned for us. In light of this, we would be wise to pursue it further, seeking to enhance our understanding and experience of this heavenly, spiritual empowerment that has been freely given to us by our heavenly Father.

Chapter 3

Spirit Travel Versus Astral Projection

Traveling in the spirit can happen in two basic ways: out-of-body and in-body. Out-of-body spirit travel is the one most people think of when they think of spiritual travel. With this method, the consciousness leaves the body with the spirit. The person experiencing this will no longer feel like he is on the physical plane, but wherever he is traveling to. This could be in the heavens, outer space, or even somewhere else in the earth, but what dictates this experience is that the consciousness travels with the spirit.

In-body spirit travel is easiest, and I suggest this is what makes up the vast majority of traveling experiences people share—including many of those in this book. When this occurs, a person's consciousness remains with his or her body. In other words, if he is sitting in a chair during the experience, he is aware he is sitting in a chair, but is engaging spiritual interaction through his imagination. The spirit journey is no less real for not being out-of-body, but it can often feel less legitimate, largely because we are trained in everyday life to believe that our imagination is completely made-up. It is a sort of linking-realm between dimensions and is designed to be the backdrop for visionary experiences such as spirit travel. We have to get used to the fact that in-body experiences are real and not just "overactive imagination," but rather *real encounters* in spite of taking place in the imagination, the movie screen of the mind.

Let me give an example of this—how we might see something in the spirit that we could call imaginary—except that this one came with a physical confirmation shortly after. Once when my wife and I were staying at a hostel in Hawaii, in the spirit I observed the spirit-form of a black woman walk down the hallway past our room. I didn't know what to make of it until either later that day or the next I passed by the front desk and saw the clerk, a young black woman, reading a book about witchcraft, at which point I knew it was her that I had seen walking past our room prior. This clearly confirmed to me that what I had seen in the spirit wasn't just a figment of my mind's making but rather was accurate—she had been astral-projecting when I had seen the form of a black woman.

The one exception to in-body and out-of-body travel is our dreams. When we dream there is no way to know how it is happening because our conscious mind is asleep and our spirit is having an experience without it, so the only way our conscious mind encounters it is as a dream. They're really just nighttime spirit-travels, but we don't typically differentiate them from other dreams.

Regardless of whether we are going to have in-body or out-of-body spirit travel experiences, we have to be able to see in the spirit to actually have those encounters—and we need to know how to interact in those encounters as well. If we don't know how to recognize, experience, and interact with visions, we will have a difficult time doing the same when traveling.

The Non-Physical Body

Many Christians want to know if traveling in the spirit is the same as astral projection, and whether we are allowed to engage in this practice as believers. While I have addressed the Biblical basis for spirit travel in the last chapter, here we will look at astral projection and spirit travel and whether they are the same or not. To do so, we must identify what they are and the mechanism(s) behind how they work.

First off, let's look at what astral projection is. *Dictionary.com* states it is, "The act of separating the astral body (spirit or consciousness) from the physical body and its journey into the universe." If we accept that we are multi-faceted beings, made of spirit, soul, and body, the concept of an "astral" body is not too difficult to swallow. It's simply acknowledging that in other non-physical aspects of our being, we still have some kind of form. Ergo the term "body." The term "astral" refers to one of two things—either the stars, or a second "body" of sorts that makes up one's aura or energy field. Energy fields are a scientific fact, known to exist. It's unarguable. The term "aura" is simply a spiritual term to refer to the same thing. We all have them, and I see them from time to time. I knew someone many years ago who saw auras somewhat regularly, and this woman was a follower of Jesus, not a devil worshipper. The reason that non-believers pay any attention to auras is because they understand that they exist in all people regardless of religious beliefs, not because of an innate desire to engage powers of darkness.

I should mention here that some people, especially followers of Jesus, try to clearly separate the spirit, soul, and body as though they all have sharp distinctions and distinctly separate functions. As a teacher I understand the benefit of breaking something down into clear systems, as many have done with the spirit-soul-body divide. When we have clear categories, it becomes easier to pass on knowledge because we have created a framework upon which a thing can be understood and remembered. And while I understand the *Bible* makes seemingly clear distinctions when it refers to the spirit, soul, and body, this model doesn't always work, and I suggest most teachings that clearly delineate between them are missing the intricate overlap between them all. The *Bible* does not clearly define the differences between them, leaving it rather open for individual interpretation. The body is somewhat obvious, as it is composed of physical matter, yet emotions, which we typically consider to be part of the soul realm, are stored inside of this physical body. Our tears of sadness have a different chemical composition than when our eyes water, as we are releasing emotions in a physical form. Negative emotions have been proven to cause physical disease as well, which doesn't make any sense if they are relegated entirely to the soul realm. Similar to this un-clarity, it is equally unclear when we discuss spirit travel if we are actually traveling with our spirit or our soul, a combination of the two, or something else entirely. According to Scripture our spirits are already seated in heavenly places (Ephesians 2:6), so does this mean when we ascend into heaven in the spirit that it is our soul, or is only part of our spirit there and another part going to meet our other half, or is there some other reality we have yet to grasp?

I have learned over the years that I can exercise not just my body, but my soul and spirit as well, and when doing so it is difficult to discern whether it is my soul, spirit, or both that are getting the workout. The Lord showed me many years ago that when we engage in prayer, we enter into a spiritual transaction of some kind, but again it has yet to be made clear whether this is with the soul or spirit, as it could be either or both. When people practice Eastern-style meditation, the energy-practices such as Qigong are designed to draw in the vital energy of the universe. Having experienced this myself, I still cannot say entirely whether this is on a soul or spirit level, although I suspect it deals more in the realm of the soul. However, many of the common manifestations of negative energy leaving the body during such practices are the *exact same* as when demon spirits leave the body during a deliverance session, so somehow this presumably *soul-energy* meditation has the ability to eject *spiritual* beings from the *physical* body. Confused yet? My point here is that the interchange between what we have termed as different "parts" is not clear by any means, and as we engage this realm further, it is entirely possible we will discover what we thought of as three clearly defined aspects of our being are really just a less-accurate way of viewing the whole. Where this relates to the idea of an astral body or spirit-body that can travel in the heavens is that we simply lack the whole picture, and almost anything imaginable is possible.

A number of schools of religious thought, some Christian and many non-Christian, believe our bodies are designed to carry more strands of DNA than the two that are identified through current research. In fact, we are beginning to discover that sometimes people have four strands of DNA in some places in their bodies (Amos)! The most common proponents of the additional-strand theory believe that we will have anywhere from three strands to twelve pairs of DNA. Many of these strands are not meant to be physical in nature, but on a more energetic or spiritual level. If we accept for a moment that we have the capacity for additional strands of DNA, some of which are not made of physical matter, we have to ask ourselves this logical question—just what do those strands of nonphysical and thus invisible DNA encode for? It doesn't take much thinking to reach the next logical conclusion—a nonvisible strand of DNA encodes for a non-visible physiology. Incidentally, science has, as of yet, been unable to sufficiently explain the existence of the meridian systems of Chinese and Japanese acupuncture, nor the chakra system of Ayurvedic medicine. Various aspects of the aura, such as electromagnetism, are able to be measured by certain scientific instruments, but ultimately what this shows is that we already possess factual knowledge of nonphysical body systems. Is it really that hard to believe that some of these nonphysical systems could contribute to an astral body?

Pastor and author Peter Tan in his book *The Spiritual World*, gives a fascinating synopsis of his trips to heaven, a document peppered with Scripture references making it easy for others to see where these realities can be found in the *Bible*. Unlike most other heaven-testimonies, this is a breakdown of his understanding of spiritual reality based on what he experienced, not simply a man telling a story of his encounter. Tan also discusses the idea of an "ethereal" DNA in this excerpt:

> Because the physical realm is patterned after the invisible realm, what we see as physical DNA (ACGT) is patterned after the invisible "ethereal/astral DNA" (EFWA) (Romans 1:20; 2 Cor. 4:18; Heb. 11:3). The ethereal/astral realm is affected by the thought energy that flows from all humans. It is also affected by the emotions and will of humans. Just as our physical bodies are constantly renewing each cell daily through our physical food; our ethereal/astral forms are constantly renewing its ethereal/astral cells through absorption of ethereal/astral life energy. Our thoughts have an effect on our ethereal/astral forms which then have a psychosomatic effect on our physical bodies. (50)

As a pastor of a large church in Asia, Tan openly acknowledges that this non-physical DNA exists, and shares additional Biblical understanding on the matter in his book, details which I won't go into here. Suffice it to say that we have a nonphysical body that is a very real and existing form we were created with. However, most of us have no clue how to use it or engage that form even though it is part of who we are and in part directs our experience on earth. Because it *is* part of how we were created, we might as well learn *how* to use it instead of running from it in fear, believing the lie that it is a false notion or New Age teaching. Tan shares another part of his encounters stating that God has the ability to do something akin to spirit travel as well, saying:

> God is able to manifest Himself in any part of the Spiritual Universe without leaving His throne. This manifestation takes a spiritual form with all the glory of God as tailored to the specific glory realm of the place where the revelation of God is unfolded. Angels and spirits in the highest spheres also possess a measure of this ability to project their presence in a spiritual form without leaving their places of abode (27).

I found it quite interesting that angels and even God can project their presence without moving their actual being, and since we are made in His image and likeness, it would make sense that we have the God-given ability to do the same. *How* we do it is another matter, but I find it fascinating that someone observed people, angels, and even God doing this very thing (or something that sounds very like it) on his visits to heaven.

In the same way that our hands are not inherently evil, although we can use them to harm or heal, our nonphysical body is not inherently evil. It is all about what we *do* with what we have been given, not whether we have it or not. God has always been more after our heart motivations which govern our actions than after the actions themselves, knowing that the things that motivate our hearts will govern our actions.

When we break all of this down, this whole astral-projection concept can be understood as simply one part of how God designed us at the beginning of creation. We each have some type of nonphysical body that comes with built-in mechanisms that allow us to travel in the spirit. The real question, then, is whether astral projection is indeed the same as spirit travel or if they are two different things entirely. Is it possible that instead of being completely different, they both use the same underlying mechanics but one has limitations the other doesn't have? To look at whether spirit travel and astral projection are the same or different, we need to look at what actually occurs when we perform each activity.

Making the Comparison

For those unfamiliar with the concept of astral projection, a silver cord is an important and necessary item to have. The silver cord is mentioned somewhat vaguely in Ecclesiastes 12:6-7, saying: "Remember him—before the silver cord is severed, and the golden bowl is broken; before the pitcher is shattered at the spring, and the wheel broken at the well, and the dust returns to the ground it came from, and the spirit returns to God who gave it." It could be likened to an umbilical cord that gives a baby ongoing sustenance, or a guide-rope that spelunkers might use when cave-exploring to make sure they can find the exit. There is a connection with the silver cord and life, and as Ecclesiastes 12 shows us, when the silver cord is severed, we die and our spirit returns to God. It is commonly known among those that practice astral projection that one must protect his or her silver cord during astral travel. Author, speaker, and close friend Praying Medic points out three main observations he discovered in his literature survey of astral projection methods and testimonies, which he elaborates on in his book *Traveling In the Spirit Made Simple*:

1. Astral projection is typically done using a method to keep the mind awake while the body is asleep. It is often done at night for this reason, but one can learn to do it through various meditative practices.
2. This process comes with a series of common occurrences—strong vibrations, loud noises, disorientation, fear, and other sensations have been reported when the consciousness or astral body is separating from the physical one, as well as at times during one's journeys.
3. There is an awareness that the consciousness has been separated from the physical body. If the consciousness remains with the body then it is not astral projection (90-91).

Additionally, anecdotal reports suggest the silver cord has limitations on how far one can travel out into the universe although it is unknown if data exists to measure the distance. Spirit travel encounters as shared by most Christians who engage in the practice do not have a distance-limitation, nor does a silver cord tend to appear in their encounters. Spirit travel includes both in-body and out-of-body experiences because one's body does not have to be asleep or in a trance-state to practice this, which is impossible with astral travel. As Praying Medic's book explains, the sounds, vibrations, and other sensations that occur when the astral body splits from the physical body do not accompany one during spirit travel because it is possible to engage in spiritual travel without the consciousness ever separating from the body (92).

While this might seem strange to some and begs the question as to whether these in-body spirit travel experiences are real, I suggest that Christians do not have the same limitations that other people have when it comes to spiritual capacity. The *Bible* says that in Christ Jesus we are a new creation (2 Corinthians 5:17), that we have been set free (John 8:36, Galatians 5:1, 2 Corinthians 3:17), and that we are no longer bound to sin and death (Romans 8:2). The Scriptures speak quite plainly regarding Jesus' desire that we would live and never die (John 3:15-16, 6:47, 11:26), how He has conquered death (1 Corinthians 15:57), and how we are no longer subject to the powers of this world (Colossians 2:15). In summary, in Jesus we have been freed from the laws that tether us to this earthly sphere and to all of the limitations that come with it, even to the point that Jesus says we don't have to die! If death is optional, then it seems perfectly reasonable that a silver cord that directly influences life and death has been made obsolete for the believer. King Solomon, who was actually a master sorcerer of his day, certainly would have known how to astral travel, so it is no surprise then that he was aware of the silver cord, yet all of his understanding was based in an Old Covenant reality prior to Jesus' redemptive work on the cross.

We have been given a promise that we will judge angels (1 Corinthians 6:3), with the *Bible* noting that we have been placed in a position of authority over them (Psalm 8:5 when properly translated). All of creation in the entire cosmos is waiting for the followers of Jesus to step into fullness as heirs of God so we can heal the universe (Romans 8:20). All of creation is meant to be subject to us, so the question becomes: are we bound to the laws of the earth, or do earthly laws become subject to us? The removal or nullification of the silver cord falls directly in line with scriptural precepts in this regard, in that even if it still exists, it no longer has the power to restrict us like it does everyone else. We have no limitations of death, time, distance, or anything else that would prevent us from traveling physically or spiritually anywhere we choose—and in those times and circumstances where we believe we are limited, oftentimes our beliefs *are* the limitation.

One point to note here is that it is entirely possible that the differences noted between astral projection and spirit travel are due to being on separate planes of existence. Peter Tan notes in *The Spiritual World* that the astral realm is the dimension of thought and imagination, whereas he differentiates the spirit realm as being a higher level of reality that exists above that. He points out that the Hebrew word *yetser*, which is often translated as *imagination*, refers to a realm of existence that contains a sort of spiritual creation of our thoughts, and that our ideas don't just exist in our minds only (54-55). The idea of *thought-forms* is a common belief in some New Age and pagan circles as well. These might be best described as pseudo-living entities created by our ideas and energy. These thought-forms often influence entire groups, such as when a community or organization is influenced by a particular fear or idea. The ongoing thoughts associated with that strong idea feed a growing astral form, which only further influences those who have bought into the notion to begin with.

This is one theory behind why cults are so effective at groupthink, because whether on purpose or by accident they cultivate an astral thought-form "hive mind" to help keep everyone in line with a certain viewpoint. This would make sense in that Psalm 103:14 uses the word *yetser* for the word *formed* when it says, "For he knows how we are formed, He remembers that we are dust." The idea that the way we are first formed is as a thought or an imagination suggests that *yetser* refers to a nonvisible body, which we could also rightly call our astral body. *If* our astral body exists on the thought-form plane, which for sake of discussion might be a lower spiritual plane than the spirit we use when spirit traveling, it would be more closely tied into the life and death of our physical body, which would explain why it is tied in with a silver cord and its limitations.

If we set aside for a moment that in-body travel is not possible with astral projection and we take into account the fact that projection is always an out-of-body experience, it seems reasonable to focus any comparison on out-of-body spirit travel. It could be said that they are two different things entirely, but I still have this feeling that they are not as different as some like to believe. Certainly there might be a difference in methodology as often when people are taken in the spirit out-of-body it is done by God or angelic forces without actively trying to engage the experience like with astral projection, but methodology alone doesn't clearly separate them as two different entities. On the other hand, lucid dreaming, where one's mind is alert and aware in one's dreams, could be considered somewhat similar to these other two practices, and might even be a sort of crossover between the two. The conscious mind is involved and the person is asleep, but he or she might or might not have done it on purpose. Some people train themselves to have lucid dreams while other lucid dreamers do not.

As said before, astral projection has limitations that spirit travel does not. This may be due to it being an actually different aspect of the nonvisible body, being an energetic form instead of spirit-body, or it could be as simple as being an unregenerate spirit-body that is still tethered more closely to the physical realm. With that said, I think it also reasonable to recognize that if one wants to learn how to spirit travel out-of-body, I'm not sure there is much in the way of training out there other than astral projection techniques. I personally don't know how to spirit travel out-of-body at will, and nothing I have read to date about the subject has provided clear guidelines on how to make this happen. The one testimony I have read that comes closest to any form of active training for out-of-body spirit travel suggests that if we practice doing in-body travel enough that we will eventually find ourselves having out-of-body experiences. To that end, practice exercises are included at the end of this book.

I will be honest, while that is something-better-than-nothing, it still isn't a good enough explanation for me. I firmly believe that if the mechanism exists, then we should be able to figure out how to activate it. Those who practice astral projection have figured out a way to activate some aspect of this mechanism in spite of the limitations that exist. While I am not specifically endorsing practicing astral projection techniques to learn to spirit travel, neither am I saying we should avoid them. It would require wisdom, Godly guidance, and then some experimentation to see if projection techniques provided anything useful regarding spirit travel training. Ultimately the mechanism exists because God designed us to be able to have out-of-body experiences, but that doesn't say anything one way or the other as to whether one *should* practice it with such an approach or not—to discover the answer will take much in the way of wisdom and discernment, and this is not a test I have conducted to date.

Regardless of whether one agrees with this author's speculations, spirit travel is a mystery the Body of Christ is gradually unraveling. I firmly believe that as time goes on, these questions that remain about the similarities and differences between astral projection and spirit travel will eventually get cleared up with answers that fully satisfy, and we will also discover how to better teach and activate out-of-body travel experiences. In the following chapter we will take a look at spiritual sight and how our ability to see in the spirit realms influences our ability to travel in the spirit.

Chapter 4

Spirit Travel Requires Spiritual Sight

In the first chapter I shared my experiences of how I learned to spirit travel largely on my own, so something both simple and foundational never occurred to me. My good friend Praying Medic mentioned an idea once while he was writing his book *Traveling in the Spirit Made Simple*—and it has stuck with me—that in order to experience spirit travel we have to be able to see in the spirit.

Before going further I do need to make a disclaimer—if we don't know how to see in the spirit it doesn't mean we cannot travel through the spiritual realms; it just means we won't be able to visually experience it unless it occurs in our dreams. And since God has designed us to be highly visual beings, it would be a serious shame for us to not have the ability to see in the spirit operating at full strength. If we don't know how to do it already, how do we learn?

To learn to see in the spirit we must first answer the question of whether it *can* be learned. Yes, it can. I suggest that all people have actually have had visions from birth forward, but fall into two groups:

those who know they have had them and those who don't yet realize it. Some people experience visions naturally and often, while others like me have had to train their awareness and ability to see in the spirit, but it is possible for everyone to experience what is sometimes referred to as *seer vision*. When we train this ability, we eventually hit a place where it becomes a common and natural part of our lives. It is possible to over-mystify this and make it seem like visions are this spooky thing that few people experience, and if they do, it comes with this otherworldly rapturous sensation. That is rarely the case although the movies would have you believe otherwise. Sometimes visions are so subtle that we can miss them if we aren't paying attention.

One example of this happened to me back in college. I was walking out of the bathroom in my apartment and for a brief moment, a fraction of a second, the picture of a deer ran through my mind. At first I thought it was strange and was going to continue with whatever I was doing, and then I realized I had just had a vision. All this takes longer to describe than the second or two in which this vision and my subsequent train of thought occurred, but because it all happened so quickly it could have been easy to miss. There was no shaft of golden light, no angelic choir, and no special sensation accompanying it—only an image for the briefest of moments that left me having to figure out what it meant. I never did, actually, as it seemed to have no discernible relevance to anything going on in my life, nor did it provide me with insight on anything to pray about. What I did learn from that encounter, however, was that we can miss things if we don't pay attention, and if we don't understand how visions most commonly occur. Maybe that was the message of that vision after all.

Sometimes it isn't an issue of learning to have visions, but not knowing what a vision actually looks like when it happens. As an adult, after learning how to experience and perceive visions, I realized that I have had visions much of my life. They were infrequent, but I never realized that those ideas and images that would sometimes go through my head were God communicating with me. From my perspective, they just seemed like I was daydreaming or had an overactive imagination. It turns out that I was having visions all along and didn't know it—nor did I find that out until years after I began training my spiritual sight. I suspect many readers are like me in that regard.

Visions can be divided into two different categories: inner and open visions. Inner visions are those that we see in our imagination or mind's eye, while open visions are those we see as though it is happening right in front of us.

An inner vision could be a simple one like with the deer—what I refer to as a snapshot vision. Snapshots are like taking a photograph, in that it is a single picture for a brief moment, and they usually only last as long as it takes for the flash on a camera to go off. Then there are moving visions that are a little more like having a scene play out in our mind. This might feel like we are just having an overactive imagination, but we have to remember that the imagination is the backdrop for visions, dreams, and prophetic experiences. Imagining something doesn't make it fake or false or not-real. The imagination is, as I said before, akin to a linking dimension between the physical and spiritual realms where information can be communicated and where we can interact with spirit beings. Throughout history, and documented clearly in Scripture, angels have appeared to people in visions to share messages from God, but these visions were just as much part of reality even though they occurred in the imagination. Beyond moving visions are interactive ones, or what I refer to as visionary experiences, where we can make choices in the vision, and where the experience includes one or more of the other senses—

touch, taste, smell, or sound. I suggest that visionary experiences verge on being a form of spirit travel or partial-travel.

Open visions can occur in the same ways as internal visions, with the main difference that the vision appears as part of or overlaid upon the world around us. A snapshot open vision might be as simple as a flash of light at the edge of our vision or when we do a double-take because we *thought* we saw something. The truth is that we *did* see what we thought we saw, but only for a moment, long enough for our minds to register what we saw, but not long enough to stare at it in detail. Moving open visions can be where the vision is interactive with the world around us, or it can appear like a movie screen in front of us that makes us unable to see our surroundings. I remember hearing a story once of a particular prophet who was playing a video game on his computer when a screen appeared in front of him and he began to have an open vision. He kept trying to look around it to see his computer monitor so his character wouldn't die, but he was unable to do so and could hear the Game-Over notification in the background as the vision continued playing before him.

It would seem to some that inner visions occur with greater frequency than open visions, but I think open visions are more common than we might think because we usually believe we are "just seeing things" when we are actively witnessing spiritual reality in a world that has taught us to ignore it. The problem, in the words of Sherlock Holmes, is that "You see but you do not observe" (Doyle). The key, then, is to practice noticing what we see and becoming mindful when we have these double-take experiences. Having visions isn't all that difficult because we all have them already, but we must learn to observe and recognize what they are when they occur. With that said, there are things we can do to enhance their frequency, as well as direct some of what and when we see things.

First, we have to understand that we have the ability to *cause ourselves* to see in the spirit. A read-through of the book of Ezekiel yields a fascinating revelation on this matter of seeing in the spirit by our own will. In the beginning of the book, the prophet frequently says "I looked and I saw" and then he shares the visions he had. Later on in the book he says that with much less frequency and more often states, "I saw." What this shows us is that the more we practice *purposefully looking* and seeing, the more we will naturally find ourselves seeing even when we aren't hunting for it. Purposeful looking basically involves a mental expectation that we will see something when we look, and it works this way for everyone, not just me. Most things in the spirit are directed by our will, which can also be termed our expectation, faith, or desire. The way this functions is that when we expect or desire something, we release faith, which is a force, to accomplish our expectation. When it comes to seeing in the spirit, our will to visualize something is what causes it to happen. Proverbs 23:7a illustrates this point by saying, "For as he thinks within himself, so he is" (*NASB*). What we think or expect within is what we cause to happen around us by releasing faith to bring it to pass. It is difficult to explain this in words because in essence we are making visions happen, but it isn't forceful—rather it is the natural outworking of spiritual functions that God created and we are simply activating them through our expectation and desire. Many people don't take advantage of this because they have never realized it is possible to search out revelation and/or see in the spirit *by choice at will* but more often than not I come across situations where I *need* to look in order to see.

Physical healing is a perfect example of this. When someone needs prayer for healing, I don't have the luxury of hoping God is going to give me revelation. I have to look and see what the spiritual problems underlying the physical malady are—but when I do, I receive the information I need to begin to address those issues in prayer.

I often see energies—swirls of black, gold, blue, red, and green are the most common. To me, each color denotes a type of problem. Black is death or disease, while red is more representative of inflammation or irritation. The color gold denotes God's glory, blue is healing energy, and green is life-energy. Yes, technically the last three are all aspects of the same things but these colors are simply the language God and I have developed to show me what He is doing in the client's body. Actually, it is more accurate to say that I picked the colors and what they mean, and when I see in the spirit, my spirit translates the relevant data into the expected colors.

I see much more than colors though. I also see demons residing in organs and tissues, as well as other demonic devices or objects—swords, knives, arrows, and all other weaponry, vices, armor, clamps, pins, screws, and other metallic-looking items that really have no place on the body. I have seen gobs of pus and goo that need to be removed, ropes, chains, other long, string-like items that I have to pull out of the person, and more. If it were in my imagination, I could just think them away and they would disappear, but I can imagine them gone all day long and they are still there in my mind's eye unless I go through the process to remove them. Sometimes this is a physical pantomiming; other times I do it in the spirit, visualizing myself remove the objects within my mind's eye. It varies from time to time how I work, but the method is the same—look with an expectation to see something, see it, and address what I see by either opposing and removing it, or helping it correct a problem. I am often fighting in the spirit against objects that appear to have sentience and resist being removed, and I sometimes have to do things in segments because I simply can't do it all at once. An example of this is that if I am removing sentient black goo, I will take the part I have gotten out so far, cut it off from the rest of the goo, seal it in a container in the spirit, and then hand it to an angel or set it down in the throne room in heaven to dispose of it, letting God do whatever He wants. With that part gone and not coming back, I then deal with the rest of the black goo. Otherwise I continually have to fight against the stuff I have removed that is running back into the wound while trying to remove new stuff, and it simply doesn't work.

I think the main reason people don't take advantage of such abilities is for the simple reason that they don't know they exist. I learned a lot about spiritual objects through trial and error and through things the Lord taught me directly—very little of it came from other people, and most of what I have heard from others has been in the past few years, a full decade after I began doing this on my own. The Holy Spirit is a great teacher, if not often a quiet one, and anything we don't know, we can ask and He will instruct us.

Seeing in the spirit is not hard, but to be successful we have to learn to trust the things we perceive. Usually these visions will be in our mind's eye—inner visions—but at times they will be open visions. Regardless of how the visual revelation comes, we have to learn to recognize it for what it is, *trust it*, and then accurately interpret and act upon what has been revealed, which is just as much part of the learning and growth process and can only be learned through ongoing practice. The frequency with which someone practices will influence how fast he or she gets good at it and will also affect how long it takes before revelation begins to come unbidden. It is a bit like training a muscle during a workout. The more one consistently exercises, the stronger the muscle becomes. Even if the workouts stop, the body has systems in place to regain what was lost faster the next time. Likewise, when we train ourselves to see in the spirit, at least part of our growth in this area becomes a permanent gain.

Engaging Visions

Many inner visions are not finite, by which I mean they are not once-and-done; we can stop them and start them up again. Sometimes when I begin to have a moving vision and get distracted, the vision either ends or my ability to focus stops, so even if it continues, I gain nothing from it simply because I can't focus enough to watch. The answer to this is to get somewhere quiet and then begin to re-imagine the part of the vision we saw last before getting cut off. While not a sure-fire solution, especially when the vision ended because of demonic interference, we can often re-enter the vision and continue from where we stopped. Activating our imagination allows us to re-enter the vision because the spiritual realms are in eternity and thus are not bound by the construct of time. The revelation was sent from eternity into this time realm, so even though the point in time is already past, if we re-imagine it, we connect with the eternal realm where that revelation still exists, and we can access it once more. As best as I can explain why this works, a good analogy is like when downloading a file on your computer. If the file download is interrupted, it will often fail and the portion of code present in the partial-file won't work properly. On the other hand, if the file completely downloads, even if we don't access it at that time, we can open it up and review it later.

Another useful aspect of this ability to re-enter visions is that we can do the same with visions that other people have. I tend to naturally do this when others are describing their visions or dreams, and I wonder how many others do as well. We naturally form pictures in our minds when we hear stories, and we do the same when we hear others share their visions and dreams. More often than not the pictures we see in our minds when someone else describes their vision or dream is not just us imagining something, but us actually *entering or re-entering the revelation.*

This ability to activate or engage our imagination to have visions is so key to spiritual sight that we need to guard the things we see with our eyes because they will influence our visionary abilities. I can only handle watching so much violence in movies before the trauma on-screen begins to affect me internally. I have learned that there are some types of movies I can't watch, even if I really enjoy the genre. Horror movies are, in my opinion, entirely off-limits for those who want to see clearly in the spirit. Certainly there are dark things out there in the spiritual realms, but the last thing we want to do is pollute our minds with garbage that is entirely fabricated and totally avoidable. I remember once when I watched only the first part of the movie *The League of Extraordinary Gentleman*. The movie has some dark overtones, and I had seen it once before, but that time I only watched the first half. I was sick that night and in my feverish state the *second half* of the movie was playing over and over again in my mind—the part I never watched. More recently I have had a similar experience, where things I was reading and focusing on invaded my imagination while I was sick, to the point that I was tossing and turning in bed as I was interacting with characters in my mind. The takeaway here is that if we have those sorts of responses when we are sick and our guard is down, then we are being affected by those same things the rest of the time; we are just less conscious of it.

I have observed a similar problem with focus especially when playing any computer game for an hour or more. If I try to spend time with God shortly after, the screen of my mind has been inundated with visual images of whatever I was playing, and I have a hard time seeing anything else. This is not to say that video games, television, or anything else electronic are evil, but that we must become aware of those things that negatively influence our ability to see in the spirit, whatever they may be. This can differ from person to person, which is why each of us must discover our negative visual triggers and adjust our daily life to alter our exposure accordingly. This isn't meant to be a legalistic rule to follow, but rather a key to help promote spiritual sight. The truth is that some things are unavoidable. If you work as a paramedic, for example, you will eventually see some really gory scenes at car crashes, and these traumatic events can emotionally and visually scar you. If you have been exposed to visually traumatic events, get some inner healing. It will both make you more whole as a person and help clear out some hefty emotional baggage that may be hindering your ability to see in the spirit.

Avoiding visual triggers can be difficult at times. When I was in college, I used to go to some friends' house every Sunday after church. The mother, Diane, was a spiritual mentor to me, and her kids were all my age, so her kids, a few other friends, and I often played volleyball in the spring and summer in their backyard, or we went inside and played cards or video games or whatever else. One time we had all just sat down to watch the movie *Elektra*. Everyone there was a believer, and there were six or seven of us present. Not thirty seconds into the beginning credits the Holy Spirit very clearly prompted me not to watch this movie. No one else understood why I couldn't watch it, and I just went and spent time alone on their back porch praying (and crying) because all I wanted to do at that moment was pretend to be a semi-normal person and just *be* with everyone else. I'm not blaming God because He was helping me with things I had asked Him to do, such as help me receive revelation more clearly, but it was upsetting at the time.

Another time I was visiting a friend in North Carolina (I lived in Pennsylvania at the time). We had gone out to the movies and had made it to the second-to-last scene of a James Bond movie when the Lord told me to leave the theater. Keep in mind I had followed the *entire plot* and the second to last scene was the final action scene! I missed the most pivotal part of the entire movie, and my friend, a missionary, didn't understand why I left either. Yes, I could explain (and I tried), but it's a bit hard to do in the middle of a theater while a movie is playing and you are continually getting a prompting from God to exit the room. I explained again after the fact but my friend still didn't understand, and some readers might not either. It all comes down to what God is doing with an individual person in that moment, and if we want to have our minds open to things spiritual then at times we will have to make sacrifices in other areas. Sometimes those sacrifices are easy and other times not so much.

Now and again we can hide or disguise these sacrificial choices and make ourselves still appear somewhat normal. Other times it will make us *that guy* in a social situation, like it did for me at my friends' house, and at the theater. Each person has to decide for him or herself how much they want to pursue this, and that includes what else he or she is willing to sacrifice in the process. On a social level, this is much more difficult to do in one's teens and twenties as an unmarried person when hanging out with friends than it is as an older individual. As people age they have other life responsibilities that creep in, peer pressure is usually a bit less, and people tend to be more understanding when life interrupts a get-together, but as a young adult the pressure is definitely there, and usually from those who are less-intense in spiritual pursuits.

I have had my own share of frustrating times when other Christians my age simply didn't understand where I was at because they were assuming I was in my walk at the same place they were in theirs, and that simply was not the case. On some level it comes down to how much we are willing to sacrifice to engage heavenly reality, but we also have to make sure to talk to Holy Spirit as we go. Doing this will save us heartache because He will lead and guide us in each situation and keep us from sacrificing in an attitude of striving without any real benefit. If we are unsure in a particular circumstance and God gives us the green light to continue, then we can enjoy the activity without stress or concern.

In the end, our ability to engage the visionary realms is of paramount importance when it comes to our experience of traveling in the spirit. While practicing seer sight is most practical for in-body travel, I believe that as we continue to exercise these abilities, it will also encourage and increase the likelihood of out-of-body travel. Nevertheless, whether in-body or out-of-body, or even outside of spirit travel entirely, the revelation we receive through visions, dreams, and other visual encounters will continue to enhance our spiritual walk, and everyone would be wise to train this innate ability.

Chapter 5

The Gift of Discernment of Spirits

The gift of discernment of spirits is vital for anyone who wants to travel through the spiritual spheres. This spiritual grace has often been boxed-in as an ability that allows us to know whether someone is speaking by the encouragement of God, one's own self, or the demonic, but it extends far beyond that simplistic usage, allowing us to perceive the presence of and understand the nature and intentions behind the various spiritual entities we encounter, and yet still more. Not everything is always as it seems in the spirit realm so this is a vitally important ability. Second Corinthians 11:14 offers a crucial warning in this regard, saying, "And no wonder, for Satan himself masquerades as an angel of light." If Satan and his henchmen can disguise themselves to appear beautiful and lovely when they are not, it stands to reason that without sufficient divine insight, any of us could be confused and led astray. Matthew 24:24 and Mark 13:22 echo this sentiment, saying, "For false messiahs and false prophets will appear and perform great signs and wonders to deceive, if possible, even the elect." The enemy actively sends spirits as well as people out to lead others astray, so we must be empowered with the gift of discernment of spirits to combat such deception.

Before diving into the gift of discernment of spirits and its relation to spirit travel, we need to take an overview of spiritual gifts as a whole. As I read it, there are three heavenly sources of gifts: The Holy Spirit, the Son, and the Father. The Apostle Paul actually mentioned these three sources in 1 Corinthians 12:4-6, saying, "There are different kinds of gifts, but the same Spirit distributes them. There are different kinds of service, but the same Lord. There are different kinds of working, but in all of them and in everyone it is the same God at work." This set of verses, while seeming to speak about the gifts all being from the Holy Spirit, actually specifies in each sentence a different personage of the Godhead—the Holy Spirit, Lord Jesus, and God the Father—highlighting that each one gives us different sorts of gifts.

Many reading this book are likely familiar with the gifts of the Holy Spirit as outlined in 1 Corinthians 12, but for those who are new to the ideas, let me give a summary. The classic verses on spiritual gifts in the *Bible* come from 1 Corinthians 12 and Romans 12, but other verses, such as Ephesians 4:11, speak of these same gifts and abilities. It should go without saying given the nature of this topic, but the doctrine of cessationism, the belief that the gifts of the Spirit ended with the early church, is incorrect. God is alive and well today and so are His gifts. A different way of looking at these abilities are to refer to them as *graces*, which is another way of translating what Paul said in 1 Corinthians 12:4. And who doesn't need more grace?

The gifts of the Son (i.e. Lord Jesus) are often referred to in charismatic circles as the "fivefold ministry," taken from Ephesians 4:11:

So Christ himself gave the apostles, the prophets, the evangelists, the pastors and teachers, to equip his people for works of service, so that the body of Christ may be built up until we all reach unity in the faith and in the knowledge of the Son of God and become mature, attaining to the whole measure of the fullness of Christ" (Ephesians 4:11-13).

If we put this together with what Paul said in 1 Corinthians 12 about the gifts of the Lord, the gifts of the Son are different kinds of service that have been bestowed as a grace upon various people so that they might *be* a gift to the rest of the Body and serve, so that *they*, the whole Body of Christ, might do works of service that God prepared in advance for them to do.

The gifts of the Father are probably even less-known than those of the Son. As it says in 1 Corinthians 12, these gifts are for different kinds of *working*, which are what we consider to be our natural talents and abilities. They are things that the Father can bestow upon us, but we're not limited to what we are born with. The *Bible* also says in Matthew 7:11 that, "If you, then, though you are evil, know how to give good gifts to your children, how much *more* will your Father in heaven give good gifts to those who ask him (*emphasis mine*)!" Another one: "Ask, and you shall receive, seek and you shall find . . ." (Matthew 7:7); and "Every good and perfect gift comes down from above, from the Father of Heavenly Lights . . ." (James 1:17). The Father definitely does give gifts, but they look a bit different from the other two. although they don't have to be any less supernatural.

The gift of discernment of spirits is a gift of the Holy Spirit and can be a bit confusing to describe because it defies simple explanation. This is because not only can it manifest itself in a variety of ways, but it differs so much from person to person that there is no simple and easy box to fit it in. I prefer to look at a series of guiding principles to help us understand how the gift *can* function. While not a guarantee, I suggest that the majority of the time we will experience this gift in ways similar to how I describe below.

First, discernment of spirits has a number of uses. As said before, it can be used to identify the source from which someone is speaking, but that is like holding a single piece of a thousand-piece puzzle and saying you have solved the whole thing. There is *so* much more to it than figuring out the source of what someone is saying. And while this aspect of discernment when combined with knowledge of the Scriptures is useful for testing prophecies, there are other applications. It can be used to discern the presence of spiritual beings, as well as their intent toward you or someone else. It can be used to discern objects in the spirit. It can be used to determine the presence of portals—doorways in the spirit realm. It can be used to discern lines of energy running between things, around things, and much more. Hebrews 5:14 says, "But solid food is for the mature, who by constant use have trained themselves to distinguish good from evil." Any of these uses are learned and developed through *constant use*. The word "senses" in that verse is the Greek word *aisthētērion* which refers to the five senses—taste, touch, smell, sound, and sight (Strong).

In the Old Testament, we see this same concept expressed using the Hebrew word *yada*. Paul Cox of Aslan's Place, a prophetic teacher and visionary, explains it this way:

> While yada is most frequently translated as 'to know', its meaning is in fact far broader. The meaning includes considered knowledge, learning, to consider, ability to distinguish, to possess a developed sense of awareness, professional skills, heightened consciousness, perception, intuition, and discernment. The physical expression of these

may include declaration and acknowledgment, performance, creativity, sexual intercourse, and skilled use of the five physical senses. (Cox)

In simple terms, this means the gift of discernment expresses itself through the senses: sight, sound, taste, smell, and touch. There is another, a "6th" sense that is a generalized internal perception that may accompany the other five. While this idea of perceiving spiritual reality through the senses can sound outlandish to some (albeit probably no more so than spirit travel), it has at times happened to people when they didn't know anything about this spiritual gift, and thus lacked understanding for their experiences.

I have experienced or witnessed all of these in my own life and in the lives of those around me. I endeavor to explain with examples some of the ways each of these can manifest. In no particular order they are as follows:

Hearing

I have heard sounds before of things that most certainly were *not* there in the physical, such as audible barking with no dogs physically present. I have heard on multiple occasions a loud buzzing/whirring or a ringing of various pitches in one ear or the other. The ringing noise always has a telltale sign right before the sound begins, as I can feel the atmosphere shift next to my ear before it starts. I have spoken with both believers and nonbelievers who have had this occur as well. While this could sound a bit like the medical condition *tinnitus* (ringing in the ears), it is actually a form of spiritual discernment although the symptoms are similar. Someone once told me it is discerning witchcraft directed at me, but I haven't found anything to substantiate or negate that claim. On the other hand, I have had times where I hear the ringing and I begin to open myself up to hear if there is a message from an angel or the Holy Spirit, and I have had both speak to me at times. I think when my ears ring, it is possible I am perceiving a spiritual wavelength that is not audible in the range of human hearing, but as I focus in I am able to hear in my heart what God and/or angels are saying to me. In a similar vein, I heard a story once of a prophet who was on a trip to Austria. On that trip the Lord allowed him to hear a top-secret conversation between Hitler and some Austrians that took place seventy years prior that had *never been put in the public record.* He announced the content of this conversation in a church meeting he held in Austria that night, and by the next day an Austrian government agency tracked him down to find out how he uncovered this confidential data. There is much more that can be discerned via hearing, but all I have shared here is just the tip of the iceberg.

Taste

I have personally never experienced this that I can recall, but I have friends who have shared their experiences with me. This manifestation involves tasting things that are *not* there and *not* presently being eaten by you. If it happens to you frequently, you will probably develop a "language" of sorts, where certain tastes mean certain things to you. For instance, a sour taste might indicate a demon and a taste of apples could represent angels. Honey might indicate the presence of God's favor, and a moldy, rotting smell could be the presence of fear. Much like dream interpretation symbols, once you know what your particular "library" of smells means, you know what is taking place in the spirit in a given circumstance.

Smell

This is similar to taste in that one can develop a personal interpretive set of smells. I have had this happen on a few different occasions. One I recall was when my college roommate Geoff was on the phone praying with a friend. Every time I walked past him, I smelled the scent of frankincense—not the essential oil, but the smell of burning incense you might smell in an Episcopal or Catholic High Church service during the Christmas season. I finally grabbed the phone and could literally smell the scent of frankincense emanating from it, with the other person still praying on the other end. Revelation 5:8 speaks of prayers as incense, saying, "And when he had taken it, the four living creatures and the twenty-four elders fell down before the Lamb. Each one had a harp and they were holding golden bowls full of incense, which are the prayers of God's people." Keeping this in mind, it is no wonder the scent I smelled during their prayers was incense as opposed to something else.

On another occasion, late at night on New Year's Eve, I joined a friend at an informal gathering from their campus ministry—we spent the night praying and prophesying over one another and stopped around 6:00 am. Sometime around 2:00 am, we began to smell hamburgers cooking. The smell was not coming from anywhere in particular, and no one in the house was cooking at that hour of the night. We had, however, discussed just prior about how God must like hamburgers, given that many of the sacrifices in the Old Testament are basically cooked meat. I think that was God having a little fun with His kids since we all smelled it. The one thing about smell that makes it more difficult to discern than taste is that it is clear whether you are eating something and can readily know if the taste is from food or not. Smell is harder because you have to figure out if you are smelling a perfume, cooking smell, or other odor that is physically present versus a spiritual scent, when all of the scent particles are nonvisible to begin with.

Sight

It will come as no surprise that this involves seeing things. One can have literal open-eyed sight (referred to as an open vision), or the kind of vision seen within the mind's eye. I usually see things in my mind's eye, what Paul calls the "eye of the heart" depending on the translation (Ephesians 1:18). I understand that what I see in my mind is actually there in front of me, but my physical eyes are simply unable to visualize it. I have seen on rare occasion something vague with my open eyes, most often a flash of light, but my wife has had open visions on multiple occasions.

Touch

Touch involves the feeling of objects or persons in the spirit. I have an old friend, Jen, who operates strongly in this aspect of the gift. To her, objects in the spirit have both physical dimension *and* weight. If there was an angel standing in front of us, I would be able to walk straight through the angel as to me it is simply empty air before us. If she tried to walk forward, she would most likely bump into the angel. Mind you, I might see that same angel in a vision, but I can move through it where to her it has solid, physical form. She used to call me when she would feel something and couldn't figure out what it was. I would look in the spirit and then either tell her what I saw or begin to describe to her what the item should feel like. Invariably, I would describe what she was feeling. As such, I say with confidence that spiritual sight and touch can pair well together when ministering. My father has described a sensation of a burning stripe of skin on his forehead when a demon is in his presence. Any time he gets that sensation on his head, it is a clear indicator to him of demonic activity taking place around him. Touch or feeling can come in a number of ways and may be very different from person to person, but again, God will help each person develop an individual discernment-language.

Perception

This perception is essentially information that is found in an internal *knowing* about something. How does one know? I can't really explain—you just know that you know that you know. This sort of download can accompany the other five senses or it can be stand-alone. When it happens to me, it typically occurs where I will get this snapshot vision but there is lots of information that is conveyed with that picture, almost like the picture is worth a thousand words but in this case the words come along with it. I don't always even have a clear view of the picture when that happens, but the information that comes with it is really what I need, so it doesn't seem to matter. I liken the images I get that carry a lot of information with them as being a spiritual equivalent of a spy-encryption method called steganography that uses an image as a way to covertly transmit data.

These six senses or means of receiving information are the primary ways one will receive revelation by way of the gift of discernment. Each sense has a number of different ways it can manifest and it will vary from person to person. I tend to get a lot of visual revelation or inner perception, but I might experience any one of them and have encountered most. This pretty much covers what I'd consider the "basics" of discernment although it's one of those topics that is so broad there is always more to learn, partly because there's always more to learn about things of the spirit.

Applying The Gift

Now that we have looked at how the gift of discernment may manifest, we need to take things a step further. It is not enough to receive the revelation—we have to apply it. When traveling in the spirit this gift is crucial because things in the spiritual spheres are not always what they seem. We cannot simply trust everything we see.

My gift of discernment most commonly operates through spiritual sight, and I have had more times than I care to count where I saw a nondescript figure in the spirit either appear nearby or begin walking toward me. I usually start off by mentally reviewing the feeling I get from it. Do I feel peaceful in its presence? Fearful? Wary and/or suspicious of it? If I get a bad vibe off of it, I don't typically wait long to send it off. Sometimes I will strike up a conversation with it in my mind, communicating spirit to spirit. When the first words out of its mouth are something like "You are going to die" or "I am going to kill you," it's a fairly clear indicator that the unidentified presence is demonic in nature. I cast them out or have my angels arrest them. At other times I may not see clearly at first but as I engage the being it appears to be okay, at least at first. If I am not sure, I continue to stay wary but watch how things play out.

One example of this was a time I had this encounter with these small, gnome-like beings. For some, the idea that gnomes exist may be anathema, but I have had enough encounters in the spirit with so-called fairy-tale creatures (elves, fairies, vampires, werewolves, unicorns, and a centaur to name a few) that I no longer question their existence—I have learned instead to discern which of them are godly and which are demonic. These gnomes were going into a hole at the base of a tree and welcomed me to come with them. Something about them just didn't *feel* right, so I continued to observe and eventually the sense of evil I got from them grew stronger. There is a difference, to me, between the feeling of darkness which carries a presence of fear with it, and the feeling of pure malicious evil. While both may be present in the same being, it seems to be a measure of either quality of evil, or a measure of the intent behind it. Certainly all beings of darkness engage in evil, but some are more self-serving and carry the aura of darkness and fear, while others engage in evil and cruelty for fun whether they derive any greater benefit or not. These gnomes felt of the latter type, and as I continued to observe, I watched them get these wide evil grins on their faces. I did not follow them into the tree.

On another occasion, I was at a friend's house when I spied another small gnome-like being, and this one was friendly. He handed me this tiny pearl-like seed, and I sensed it was meant to bless me in some way. And while I forget what I did with the seed at the time, this figure lacked the sense of malice and of things just being *off* in some way, feeling peaceful instead. I gladly accepted this one's gift. Discernment of spirits is what helps us differentiate between spirit beings that may look similar on the exterior, but who are nothing alike on the inside.

Probably the strangest being I have ever discerned was back in 2006. I was at a church in the media booth with the sound guy and we were praying together. I saw this basketball-sized meteor-like object fall in our midst and this strange-looking baby crawl out from inside it. I still don't know what it was there to do, but that thing was strange and demonic all at once, and I sent it off.

While spirit travel might seem innocuous on the one hand, and in many cases it is, as we go deeper into the spiritual realms, whether we are in body or out-of-body, real dangers exist. Our spiritual bodies can be attacked, and while we might not sustain physical damage, spiritual wounds are real and can cause problems. Back in 2007 my wife and I were pushed into a situation where we were fighting a coven of witches, among other things. I go into more detail in Chapter 10 discussing spiritual combat, but when all was said and done, I lost a lot of my internal drive for things spiritual. This continued for some time—a direct result of the enemy attack. In a worst-case scenario presumably one could die when engaged in things spiritual, but if your spirit got trapped somewhere in the spiritual spheres, it is possible that the problems would not end with bodily death.

The goal of sharing this is not to scare people away from spirit travel although for some that might be the knee-jerk reaction. It is God's desire and design for us to engage the spiritual realms, so avoiding them really isn't a long-term option. In fact, I believe anyone who tells people to avoid spirit travel because there are risks is badly misguided. That's like saying we can get burned by fire, so we should never light candles, have fires in a fireplace, or use gas stoves. Never mind that many houses are heated using gas, which requires a pilot light. Basically, if you should avoid traveling in the spirit because it could be dangerous, you should probably also stop heating your home and cooking food because somewhere, somehow, sometime, someone got hurt. No matter that *not-cooking* some foods would be far more harmful, or that freezing to death is also fatal. Likewise, we have to be consistent with how we engage things spiritually. We are in a long-term spiritual battle. Injury and problems are *literally impossible* to avoid. Sure, using wisdom and good judgment will help us avoid certain problems, but they can't keep us from all harm ever. Avoiding traveling in the spirit out of fear is foolish at best, and at worst we will miss out on aspects of our destiny that God planned for us from before the foundations of the world. We *must* learn to use discernment and wisdom, not so we can shy away from spiritual encounters, but so we can navigate them well.

Chapter 6

Oh The Places You'll Go!

Congratulations!
Today is your day.
You're off to Great Places! You're off and away! You have brains in your head.
You have feet in your shoes. You can steer yourself any direction you choose.
You're on your own. And you know what you know. And YOU are the guy
who'll decide where to go...
... And will you succeed?
Yes! You will, indeed! (98 and ¾ percent guaranteed.) KID, YOU'LL
MOVE MOUNTAINS! So ... be your name Buxbaum or Bixby or Bray
or Mordecai Ali Van Allen O'Shea, you're off to Great Places!
Today is your day! Your mountain is waiting. So ... get on your way!
- Dr. Seuss in *Oh The Places You'll Go* -

When we travel in the spirit, there are a variety of places we can go, both nonphysical and physical, in the heavens and the earth. Spirit travel can take us into the realms of the heavens, which means not just the Paradise of God where the Throne is located, but through the various spiritual spheres both light and dark, what we commonly refer to as heaven and hell. It can also take us around the world and out into the cosmos—off the planet and into the stars.

In March of 2006, Peter Tan, pastor and author of the book *The Spiritual World*, was taken into a series of visitations to heaven, where he was shown a broad scope of "how things work" (5). I have read many different testimonies of people's encounters in heaven but his are by far the most comprehensive, explaining the heavenly realms from a much broader perspective than most. As he describes it, the spirit realm is much more vast than something that looks like our universe—full of space with only a little actual "stuff" here and there. The heavens are also far more than a single, massive landmass. Rather, they are a series of universes or spiritual spheres that have varying levels of glory or heavenly light associated with them, and these spheres make up all of creation, both physical and spiritual. They range from dark to light, and many are spheres surrounding other spheres—with different levels of reality at each level. There are multiple levels, which Tan breaks into three categories: planetary, celestial, and God-spheres (25-26).

A rough example of what this could look like is matryoshka dolls—small figurines that sit one inside another, also called nested dolls. Imagine that the physical world has a soul/spiritual sphere around it, with a celestial one around that and an even higher sphere around that one. But to make matters more confusing, it's almost like a bunch of marbles inside a plastic egg, with a series of marble-filled plastic eggs inside a basketball—wheels within wheels within wheels, akin to the imagery show to the prophet in Ezekiel 1:15-16. Then put a series of these basketballs in a line in a room with a window on one end and darkness on the other end. The basketball in the middle of all of these spheres is the one containing our earth. As you can see, the spirit world is a complex intertwined series of higher and lower realities.

Using this example, the ones heading toward the shadows are what we think of as hell—a series of realms filled with spiritual beings who are steeped in darkness. Some of these beings are demons and others are humans who have yielded to dark inner desires and demonic influences during their lifetimes. In the other direction, the marble-filled-egg-filled basketballs toward the bright window are the celestial spheres that are filled with saints, angels, and all manner of other God-fearing creations. They constantly absorb and reflect God's heavenly light down toward all of the darker spheres to spread God's love and light to us.

The reason this is important is that based on many conversations I have had with people about the heavenly realms, many people believe they are a simplistic linear invention that is extremely easy to understand. God is complex beyond compare, and the many worlds He has formed are intricate and complicated. People have used Paul's statement in 2 Corinthians 12:2 where he speaks of the Third Heaven, in conjunction with other passages, to simplify all of heavenly reality into three heavens—our atmosphere as the First Heaven, an Intermediate Realm filled with angels and demons as the Second Heaven, and then the Paradise of God as the Third Heaven. The *Bible* says in Deuteronomy 10:14 that, "To the LORD your God belong the heavens, even the highest heavens, the earth and everything in it." Heaven has levels—both the heavens *and* the highest heavens—which are somehow a step above the normal ones. Some translations say the "heavens of heavens." And while some might separate these two heavens into outer space and some sort of spiritual realm outside of that which we think of as where God lives, it has never been that simple.

Consider this—if there are only three realms, earth, outer space, and heaven, then where is hell located? Where did the imprisoned souls that Jesus preached to in 1 Peter 3:19 go to *be* in prison? What about the Abyss referred to in Revelation 9:2? Are we to assume that these spiritual beings are imprisoned somewhere deep inside the physical earth? That's about the only thing that doesn't make sense—that physical rock is somehow an adequate prison for spiritual entities that can travel through matter. No, the spiritual realms are so incredibly vast that if we filled the entire world with books of knowledge about it, we would not have touched on more than a small fragment of all that there is to know. My friend Hope, a prophetess, told me a story once of a vision she heard a minister share. In this vision Jesus was standing on a beach rolling a single grain of sand between his fingers. The message in this encounter was that if all the sand in the world is the fullness of God, our collective knowledge and revelation as humans about God only makes up the equivalent of a single grain of sand. If God is that expansive, it is illogical to think that the heavens He created are any less extensive.

The Heavens

Regardless of where one travels in the celestial realms, God's glory is shining from his throne into that place. A location may be so incredibly steeped in darkness that just a vague fraction of a sliver of a tiny bit of that light makes it there, and that little bit may be shut out for a time by the residents there, but God's spiritual light surpasses and overcomes all darkness. John 1:5 says, "And the light shines in the darkness, and the darkness did not comprehend it." The word translated as *comprehend* is the word *katalambano* which means *to apprehend, lay hold of, seize, or take possession over.* Only one part of that meaning is *to lay hold of with the mind* which could be understood as *comprehend* (Strong). That verse is probably better translated to say that "the light shines in the darkness, and the darkness could not seize, apprehend, or take possession or control over it." In simple terms, the powers of darkness are incapable of stopping Gods' light.

Sure, they might be able to block some of it for some time, but they cannot stop all of it for all time—which means even in the deepest reaches of the depths of hell, the powers of darkness simply cannot prevent God's glory from invading and taking over.

While this might seem a bit of a sidestep regarding travel in the spirit, we need to understand that when the *Bible* says in Psalm 115:16 that, "The heavens are the heavens of the LORD, but the earth He has given to the sons of men" (*NASB*) it means *all the heavens* are God's domain and property. Hell might be somewhere that God has let Satan and the forces of darkness hang out for a time, but He has no intention of letting it remain that way forever. God's love and goodness are so invasive and irresistible that when it says in Phillipians 2:10-11, "That at the name of Jesus every knee should bow, in heaven and on earth and under the earth, and every tongue acknowledge that Jesus Christ is Lord, to the glory of God the Father" it means that everyone will bow *willingly*, not because God forces them to. Romans 14:11 says the same thing, quoting Isaiah 45:23. God's love is relentless, and where it says in 1 Corinthians 13:8a that "love never fails," God's love truly does not fail, which means that eventually, at some point outside of this time-realm, even Lucifer the fallen angel will eventually be saved when he calls upon the name of Jesus, because Jesus was the slain lamb in eternity for those who sinned and fell away there, and for all who will come to know Him outside of time.

While this is a somewhat controversial belief, and this might be the place where someone is tempted to scream "Heresy!" and throw this book as far away as possible, I encourage you to keep reading— I am going somewhere with this. When people think of "universalist" heresy, it is often based on the idea that anyone can get to heaven whether they accept the sacrifice of Jesus or not—that is nothing like what I am talking about. Jesus is *the* only way to the

Father, and he was quite clear about that in John 14:6 when he said, "I am the way and the truth and the life. *No one comes to the Father except through me (emphasis mine)*." The issue most people struggle with here, and which is the matter I am discussing, is whether we can come to Jesus after death or not, not whether one can get to heaven regardless of what they believe. There is a really good book by Richard Murray titled *The Question of Hell* (found at www.thegoodnessofgod.com) which addresses this from the perspective of the first five centuries of the Church, who maintained this doctrine, known as *apokatastasis*, until outsiders came in with pagan beliefs and altered things to where we have them today. It was actually the common belief of the church for *centuries* that God's redeeming power does not end at death, and that belief was based on the Scriptures. Any claim of heresy in this area must be evaluated based on the original perspective of the early church before pagans came in and perverted end-times doctrine until it reached its current form.

The reason any of this matters at all for the sake of spirit travel is that *all* of the heavens, even those areas steeped in darkness, belong to God, and as His heirs we have access to all of them. This means that we can travel to Heaven, Hell, or anywhere in-between. While I suggest it is foolish to try to convert demons in hell unless Jesus confirms to you in a myriad of different ways and then *personally escorts you there Himself*, it is still important to know that we have access anywhere.

For clarification's sake, I will refer to the darker, demonic-filled spiritual spheres as Hell or Hell worlds, and the ones that are filled with God's glory and light as the Celestial worlds, although in fact all are technically part of the heavens. The various Celestial worlds have levels with greater and lesser glory—although in talking about places of "lesser glory," they all still surpass the level of God's glory we experience here on earth by far. When we travel through these

Celestial realms, we can engage the myriad of spiritual beings who reside there, as well as the various benefits of those places.

One example of this is a time God took me through some inner healing. I was in a worship service at the ministry school I had gone to over a decade ago, when I went in the spirit to the place I first learned to visit the heavens, the field with the tree. This particular visit wasn't something I planned—it just happened.

At any rate, I was standing in this field and started walking, and then I was running down this road. As I was doing this, a white horse literally emerged from the ground underneath me and all of a sudden I was seated on it as it ran at massively high speeds. I really couldn't see anything that we were rushing past until we arrived at the gates to a city, with two men standing there, one on either side of the gate. The road was a dirt road right up until we reached the city, and right at the edge of the city it became paved. I dismounted the horse and as soon as I stepped onto the pavement, my garments changed from whatever I was wearing into priestly garments.

The two men at the gate let me pass and I entered this city. There was a road in front of me that led uphill, with a fountain in the middle. Jesus was there and He placed me in the fountain, the water running over me, washing me completely. Next, He led me to the right down a short street and into a short building—like a one-story house or something. Anyway, He took me into a room and stripped off my clothes, then began to pour oil from a jar all over me until my body was dripping completely with this oil. After that He held His hands over me and blood began to pour from His hands and run all over my body as well. Essentially I had been bathed in water, then oil, then His blood. I was thinking I was still naked (which overall the experience was kind of strange), but Jesus simply told me to look down and as I did so I was amazed. The oil and blood had formed this dark-colored almost-black skintight suit that covered my entire body—almost like a wetsuit or spandex bodysuit might look. In other words, I was clothed with whatever mixture He had covered me with. I don't recall whether I was taken back to the field or not, but the experience basically ended there.

What I found so unique about this encounter wasn't just the oddity of the event itself, but the results I observed in the natural realm. Whatever Jesus had done altered my internal emotional state. As best as I could tell, the body-suit Jesus covered me with was responsible for this outcome, although He did some inner healing at the time as well. This was a profound experience for me, and one that is still pretty cool as I think about it, because it was proof-positive early on for me that spiritual encounters can have literal physical effects in this realm. When we travel to the heavens we aren't simply imagining things that have no influence on the outside world but can directly impact earth "as it is in heaven." If you want to travel to a similar place, start by imagining yourself at a large white fountain with a geyser in the center, and see what God does from there. I can't guarantee a spandex bodysuit for the occasion, but whatever happens will be a good thing.

One of the things I always find perplexing when hearing others share their spirit journeys is when they ask if someone has been to a specific location. As explained, the heavens are incredibly vast—one can travel to different parts of the heavens in a variety of spiritual spheres. It seems incredibly silly to me to hear someone say "Have you ever been to the library", or wine cellar, or whatever other location they mention, not because they don't exist—they do. It's just that within the myriads of Celestial worlds, do we really think there is only one library and a single wine cellar? There is at least one desert-like area that is made entirely of gemstones of various sizes, to the point that each grain of "sand" is a tiny stone. I like to call it the Gemstone Desert. I have only been to the one, but I generally assume there are a number of those in various places. Prophetess Kat Kerr, in her book *Revealing Heaven: An Eyewitness Account*, speaks of an amusement park, but even on earth we have hundreds of them in the USA alone. I have personally seen cities, a castle floating in the sky, a massive rainbow that dwarfs anything we have seen here on earth with hues that are far more vibrant than any earthly tone, and more. I find it incredibly unlikely that only one of each of these exist in the *entire heavenly realms*.

I once knew a woman, Annette, who had a heavenly encounter where she and her ministry team were all taken in the spirit together. When they went to travel from one layer of the Celestial realms to another, they went up and down in a whirlwind, almost like it was an elevator. 2 Kings 2:1a says, "When the Lord was about to take Elijah up to heaven *in a whirlwind (emphasis mine)*. . ." While I am certain there are other means of spiritual transport, I do find it interesting to note that the Scriptures do corroborate that whirlwinds are a valid means by which one might ascend or descend from various levels of heaven.

Once when I was at that same field I began my journeys at, I found a host of angels flying around in the air above the field. I joined them in playing something akin to a combination between tag and dodgeball, which was incredibly fun. We flew around in the air, tossing these balls of light at one another. One in particular that I recall was when an angel and I dropped a light ball on an angel flying beneath us. He fell down and, given it was heaven and nothing is hurt or harmed there, he was not injured—it was hilarious at the time. I find it interesting, in light of this heavenly encounter, that in the Harry Potter series there is a popular Wizarding game called Quidditch which in some ways sounds very much like this—people flying around and throwing balls at one another. That's not to say that Harry Potter is somehow the gold standard for heavenly experiences, but I do believe that we see glimpses of heavenly realities communicated to us in books and movies, even secular ones, far more often than we realize.

The Cosmos

The heavenly realms are not the only places we can travel to outside of earth—we can travel to the cosmos as well. The cosmos, scripturally, can be defined as the entire universe, as well as the hosts of heavenly beings in it, divine government, and the inhabitants of earth. In other words, it includes everything in this physical realm. The *Bible* says a lot more about it than we think. In Mark 16:15 Jesus instructs the disciples to preach the gospel to every creature in the cosmos. Luke 9:25 asks the question of whether it is of any benefit if a man gains the cosmos but loses his own soul. John 1:9 says that Jesus is the true light that comes to everyone who is brought into the cosmos. Again in John 3:17 it says that God brought Jesus into the cosmos not so He could condemn it, but to redeem it through him. If the word *cosmos* is too unfamiliar, just substitute the word *universe* in there and you will get the idea.

God is all about redeeming all of creation, not simply planet earth. While I cannot prove or disprove scientifically the existence of life on other planets, I do suspect there is far more sentient, God-created life out in the universe than we have any concept of, and I also believe God has ordained for us to repair the damage that has been done to star systems. Take the asteroid belt, for example. Why on earth is there a ring of broken stone and debris floating around in the middle of our solar system? The only reason it is a ring now is due to the ongoing rotation of the solar system causing it to spread out over time. Since we know it must have spread out over time, what would it have looked like if it was *not* spread out? Basically it would be a mass of rock gathered in a clump. Interestingly, a massive clump of rock that orbits a star is usually called a *planet*—which is what I suggest the asteroid belt used to be at some distant point in the past prior to its complete annihilation.

Madeline L'Engle was a mystic who saw and experienced far more of spiritual reality than we have any concept. In chapter 6 of her book *A Wrinkle in Time,* two characters, Ms. Whatsit and the Happy Medium, show the main characters a star going supernova—exploding in a burst of power to combat powers of darkness out among the stars. I have had spirits of various stars visit me before, one time showing up from Orion's Belt to speak to me in my driveway. The stars are much more involved in our lives than we think.

Exodus 20:4 was given as a command to the Israelites for a reason: "You shall not make for yourself an image in the form of anything in heaven above or on the earth beneath or in the waters below." This command only makes sense if indeed there *are* forms in the heaven above, on the earth, or in the waters to make images of. And while it is easy to assume that these images are being fashioned after animals in the sea or on the earth, there isn't anything they could have referenced to make images of the heavens—especially since the people of Israel didn't have telescopes or satellites and had not yet sent robots to other planets. In spite of this, the images worshiped most often in the Old Testament are of beings in the heavens including the sun, moon, and stars.

If we really think about it, the Israelites and those of other cultures of that time period must have known something we don't currently understand. I mean, what are they going to do, make an altar to a really tiny blinking dot in the sky, and then another altar to the blinking dot next to it, complete with animal and child sacrifices just for no reason? I don't think anyone is that silly. Since they were making altars and sacrificing humans and beasts alike to these spirits, they had to have known something other than what modern science tells us—that there are indeed spirits who live out in the cosmos.

With all this in mind, consider the encounters that people of ancient times must have had with spirits of the sun, moon, spirits of other planets, and all the "Starry Host"—what I refer to as *stellar spirits*. And if all of these otherworldly places have spirits, what is stopping the earth from being ruled or otherwise dominated by a spirit as well? What if there is indeed a single spirit that is ruling over this planet? After all, the term "Mother Earth" has been around for a while, and there are many cultural traditions that acknowledge that the earth itself has a spirit. While I am not suggesting we hunt down some Planet-Earth Spirit, I find it no great surprise that people throughout history in their naïveté of God have worshiped the sun, moon, and stars, because at its very base this points to the fact that there indeed *are* spirits that govern aspects of the stellar sphere. And if there are spirits there, then it seems reasonable that occasionally people might interact with them.

Humans have interacted with these stellar spirits in the past, and if it has happened before it will happen again. As Solomon himself said in Ecclesiastes 1:9, "What has been will be again, what has been done will be done again; there is nothing new under the sun." Ephesians 3:10 states "His intent was that now, through the church, the manifold wisdom of God should be made known to the rulers and authorities in the heavenly realms." If God expects us to reveal His wisdom to rulers and authorities in the heavens, we might actually have to interact with the rulers and authorities of the heavenly realms. This brings us to the inescapable fact that at least some of us are going to encounter these stellar spirits at some point, and if we don't personally, we will meet other people who will. But that's not all; the *Bible* says more on the subject.

Ephesians 1:9-11 says, "And he made known to us the mystery of his will according to his good pleasure, which he purposed in Christ, to be put into effect when the times will have reached their fulfillment – to bring all things in heaven and on earth together under one head, even Christ." Somehow, God purposed through Jesus to bring *all things* under Jesus, not just people, and in all locations in existence. This means that through some yet-hidden means, all things *in heaven* and on earth will be brought together under one head, and I can only imagine that God has revealed to us the mystery of his will because He wants us to take part in it. If you read just a few verses prior to the one above, you will read that God has adopted us as sons through Jesus and has blessed us with every spiritual blessing in heavenly places as a result. This means that we, as co-regents, co-heirs, and co-laborers with Him must not only engage in heavenly places to access the blessings located there, but also will have some part in the bringing together of all things.

To whet your appetite for the *more* that God has in store for you in this area, I want to share a testimony with you. My good friend Hope was taken by the Lord on a three-and-a-half hour journey out into the universe, and she has graciously allowed me to share it here:

> Somewhere around 1990 I was at a meeting at a friend's house, one of the friends whom I traveled with at that time. There were eight to ten people there in total in this large room with a wood-burning stove. I got up from the chair I was sitting in to get a *Bible* or something that was across the table. I walked across the room, and when I bent over to reach forward to grab the item, my one foot was raised in the air behind me and I was completely off-balance. That was the moment the trance started and I began to have this visionary experience, totally frozen in place.

Through the whole encounter I was narrating where I was, saying, "Oh, I'm going into this" and would explain what I was entering.

I traveled through twelve separate dimensions, different planes of existence. The second dimension I went through was very dark; rocky shale-filled ground, almost as if I was diving deep into an underground cavern. The rocks were wet and damp with a lot of recessed caves; pitted like one might imagine an asteroid surface to look like. It was very dark, damp, moldy, and demonic. I was on a white horse with a really pretty mane, riding bareback. All the caves had these dark figures, demonic entities in them. As I passed by, these figures in the caves would shrink back so I was unable to reach them. I didn't want to touch any of them, but they were hiding away from me as if they were scared because they knew who I was. I remember feeling very sad while going through that dimension, and I watched as they withdrew into their dark, deep holes. There were hundreds upon hundreds of them, and I can see that part clearly to this day. That dimension was the only realm I was on a horse.

I remember hearing the group around me talking as I was going through this dimension, and they said, "You need to go with her, you are a Levi and she is a Judah, and you need to cover her as she goes through this experience." When this man stepped up next to me he also went into the trance, because he began to see what I was seeing. I don't remember all the dimensions. One that was right after the encounter with all the caves in the tunnel was so stunning it was as if I was in the fields of heaven, so beautiful that I can't describe it very well. The one place was like earth but one hundred times brighter and more brilliant and stunning. What I remember was flowers of every color that I can think of. It was very bright and colorful; there were trees, and it was just this awesome, wonderful feeling wherever I was. It is so difficult to describe I'm not sure if I walked or flew, but it seemed like I was down near the ground, as if I was in Yosemite Valley, filled with waterfalls and flowers; peaceful and beautiful. I can't really describe it, but I will never forget it. The whole feeling in that place was wonderful, and it was gorgeous, filled with peace, joy, love, and I was like "Aaah, wow!" This land was pristine and untouched; no cars or technology or signs of human touch, almost like one might imagine you would find in a fairy tale.

It wasn't a gradual change from one place to another, but each time I came into another dimension it was a brand new thing; almost like flipping the page of a picture book to see something entirely new. It was always a drastic change and it felt really difficult to comprehend; it seemed like it was just a few seconds at one place and thirty seconds in another. One of the dimensions after that beautiful realm felt like I was in outer space, with things flying toward me or going around me, almost like I was flying through nebulas and through asteroid belts and stuff, but I had perfect peace because I knew nothing was going to hit me. It felt like someone was holding my hand leading me through. It was kind of fun, actually.

One of the more strange ones was this dimension where I felt like I was on the motherboard of a computer. It was all very foreign to me, but very techie—almost like I was inside electronic circuitry. I just kept going through it and looking at all the details. I remember saying to myself "What is this?" The man who was with me was a real techie guy, and he was like, "Oh, it's like you are inside the motherboard of a computer." I remember that one because it was so strange.

Eventually he got scared and said, "I've gotta go back, I've gotta go back. I can't go any farther."

"I said, "No, there's a purpose for this. God is sending us here for a reason, we have to keep going."

He said, "No, I can't. I can't, I have to go back." He was scared; I don't know why. I think it was the first time he had experienced anything like that and was overwhelmed. Right then God showed me hundreds upon hundreds of ice cream cones. For whatever reason, God talks to me in ice cream cones. Every flavor, every kind. I never touched them, but my entire vision was filled with these ice cream cones, and they were a sign to me that I was where God wanted me to be and doing what He wanted me to do. God gave me this sign to keep going and not to be scared—I was in his will. I said "No, we're there, we're there!" but he left at that time and went back. I can still see that ice cream so distinctly.

Right after he left, the ice cream cones disappeared and I flew in horizontally to this group of people, almost like a hovercraft. I knew this dry, desert-like area was where I was supposed to be. These people were all in dark brown robes with their faces covered and their heads down; I couldn't see their faces. I felt like they had been in chains for eons, as a group of people who don't age like we do, and who had been in existence for a long, long time, but had been in chains for very long as well. There were these dark, smoky figures, black shadows like you might see in the corner of your eye when you see something demonic. They were interspersed among these people. I began to shout suddenly, "Seek ye first the Kingdom of God! Seek ye first the Kingdom of God!" over and over again. I couldn't stop shouting it, but as I did this, the demonic figures began to pull back. They withdrew and the people were set free.

The leader of this community of people was a tall and dignified older man with graying hair; strong, not feeble. He was a sturdy figure standing out in front of the group. There were men and women of all different ages in that crowd, but I did not see any children. Their faces changed from being ashen with the pallor of death, oppressed, and frightened— their eyes started shining and their countenances completely changed. They were free. This group of people had been totally oppressed, and when I shouted, light came upon their faces and they were set free. It was like the chains had fallen off and they were no longer in bondage. I knew they were feeling God's love, and I was feeling God's love for them. I don't know who they were, but they were free. I remember the head man thanking me, and I just told them not to thank me, but to thank God. I'm not sure if they were actual people or just representative of people or what, but I knew they were free. After that I knew I was done—I had completed my mission.

It was very exciting because I knew God had freed those people, but I didn't know where they were. I just knew they were in total bondage and being oppressed, and as I was quoting the Scriptures, the demonic dissipated and withdrew from them. The light came in and it was amazing to watch the change on their faces.

Now that this encounter was over, I was so drunk in the spirit that I had forgotten my glasses at the house the prayer event was at. I couldn't drive and friends had to drive me home. I had thought I was only gone for five to fifteen minutes, but then my friend's husband told me, "You were gone for three and a half hours, narrating each dimension as you went." It was impossible for me to stand in that position for three hours or more one foot in the natural and I wouldn't have believed it had been that long if it hadn't been for a room full of witnesses (Personal Interview).

Hope's spirit travel encounter yields varied and interesting information. Before going further I should mention that Hope is a very mature believer, having followed the Lord for nigh on fifty years, and she is no stranger to supernatural encounters. The first thing of note is that in this experience, she wasn't just somewhere in the heavenly realms but rather traveling in and through multiples of dimensions. We touch on this idea of multidimensional travel again in the next chapter, but this encounter makes us consider that other dimensions both exist and that we are able to travel to and through them in the spirit. Her travel through the dark cave-world filled with demonic beings suggests that not every area is safe to be in, but of note is the fact that those entities were afraid of her, not the other way around. That should tell us something about our authority in the spirit as sons and daughters of the Living God.

Next, we know from the encounter that she was traveling in the spirit and not there bodily because witnesses were there and physically saw her body remain present in the room for the entire trip, with another man able join her partway through the journey. While it might seem odd to some that God would send someone on cross-dimensional spirit travel, it seemed that God's main purpose here was to bring deliverance to an ancient race of people who had been in captivity to the demonic realms for some time. While the exact details of where and when this occurred are impossible for us to know, it is clear from the encounter that the Lord had a specific mission for her, and that in following through no matter how strange things got, Hope was able to see the mission through and set the captives free—just like Jesus.

Some might find it hard to swallow that there is other life out there or that other dimensions exist, but the truth is that the *Bible* tells us we are made a little lower than God and will judge angels someday. Is it that difficult to believe that we might also be governing other races of people? Jesus told his disciples to preach the gospel to the cosmos, and in declaring the Word of the Lord in this situation, Hope did exactly that. No matter how odd things might get, God has divinely ordained that we, the heirs of the promise of redemption through His Son, might work to bring all things under His feet, and if there is rebellion out there among the stars, then it will eventually fall to us to help bring that under His dominion as well.

The Earth

If we consider that we can travel to and fro among the heavens and the cosmos, why not the earth? Wouldn't it seem sensible that we might travel back and forth in the earth, doing good deeds? This is a very real possibility, and something that happens more often than we realize. We will discuss a little more in the next chapter about ministering to others in our dreams, but many of my friends and I have traveled throughout the earth during spirit travel encounters. Of particular note are Hope's encounters ministering to people via spirit travel while she was awake during the daytime. Because all of these stories are out-of-body spirit travel, it is impossible to know if she was physically there or if she went in spirit only, but regardless of how the miracle occurred, these stories represent just a small portion of what is available to us as we engage this ability and learn to steward it well.

The following two stories are again from my dear friend Hope, who has not just traveled into the heavens in the spirit, but whom the Lord has brought on journeys around the world as well. She shares:

> One early afternoon I was sitting in my family room. The Lord asked me if I would go to a prison cell in the Middle East to rescue someone, a soldier. I didn't know where, exactly, but it was in the early 2000s after we had gone to war in Afghanistan and Iraq. I found this to be a strange question because I had already told God in the past that I would do anything and go anywhere He wanted me to go, and He had done just that! I asked Jesus, "Why are you asking me?"
>
> He said, "Because of the danger of the situation." It was then that the Lord revealed to me in a vision what danger I was facing, as well as the fate that would befall this soldier if I didn't go to rescue him.
>
> When Jesus showed me what they were going to do to this man, I had a nanosecond of fear which I had never had before, almost like "If they are doing that to him, what would they do to me if they caught me?" Before I let the fear take hold, and as quickly as it came on, I said, "Yes, I will go." I then thought to myself, "How am I going to teach him to transport out?"
>
> I remember the Lord saying before I went "Tell him I have sent you to him like I sent Phillip to the Ethiopian Eunuch," then I disappeared from my living room.
>
> I remember it was dark, presumably at night, when I appeared in a horrible-smelling room. The cement and ground were all wet, like I was in a basement or cellar of some kind. Dogs were barking, and I heard men talking in a

language I did not understand. I was inside a prison cell, and there in front of me was a soldier on his knees praying. I didn't know this at the time, but later when I described his uniform to a friend with some expertise in this area, he told me, "It was the army; he was chaplain."

This soldier was on his knees crying and praying and I had literally just appeared to him in the cell. When he saw me, he stood up, and I said, "Jesus has sent me to you like He sent Phillip to the Eunuch in Ethiopia." Then I thought "Now what do I do?" At that moment the Lord instructed me to take this soldier's hand in mine. The moment I did so, we were suddenly transported to an office with five desks— a military office with large glass windows and a hallway. This one good-looking soldier stood up and he said the name of the man I had just rescued. He said, "So and so is here; he's in the office!" One of the other men behind the desk ran down the hall screaming "He's here" and was yelling this chaplain's name. It got crazy in there very fast, as it seemed like everyone knew he had been captured. I remember the shocked looks on their faces—I want to laugh and cry at the same time when I think of it because it was all just so astounding to them. The one man was partway standing up and he was just so stunned it was like he couldn't move. Right after that, God took me out. I was like "Wait, I don't remember his name!" I wanted to go back and watch what happened after that, but I was unable to.

While I don't know for sure if I was there in body or not, as I had been alone in my living room when I left, this event is hard for me to forget, partly because that was the first time I ever had that moment of fear. The Lord has taken me on so many different journeys and I had never been afraid before. It was this really strange feeling to me. Yet, God was faithful to protect me, and as soon as I said, "Yes," I was out of the family room, gone to the other side of the world. During the whole experience, my main question was "Why did he ask me to go?" I never used to understand why, but later a friend told me that I used to do it by obedience, but that now God wanted to partner with me in this instead of me just going where directed.

Another time, I was taken in the spirit to the border of Israel and Lebanon, in an area of thick trees. I met two Israeli soldiers there and began sharing with them about Jesus being their Messiah. I forget the exact number, but while we were talking either seven or fourteen Hezbollah soldiers came charging toward us and the pair of Israeli soldiers turned and ran. I turned around and said to myself, "No, this is not going to happen." I took up my sword of the spirit that was at my side and even as I looked at these Hezbollah soldiers I could see demons over top of every one of their heads. I have had a diamond sword in the spirit before, but this time it looked just like a normal steel blade. I never touched the humans, but made one slash through the crowd of demons above them.

As I cut the heads off the demons over top of these soldiers, I watched all of the soldiers' heads fall off at the same time. It kind of freaked me out, and I didn't understand why the Lord would let me cut peoples' heads off. I asked the Lord what was happening and He said, "What you do in the spiritual realm manifests in the natural." I am still not entirely sure if it actually happened in the natural or not, but at first I always thought it was only in the spirit, but after I had friends see my body disappear when the Lord took me places at times, I began to wonder if maybe the soldiers truly had been decapitated.. If nothing else, it was a lesson for me that what we do in the spirit realm is powerful, and has the ability to manifest in the natural. I didn't have television at the time, but I asked a friend who did have access to the news if that situation had come up. I never did find out, but that used to happen often with myself and the group I traveled with—where what we did in the spirit realm would appear the next day on television.

These two stories, while both military in nature, show us that it is possible to be taken in the spirit, whether in-body or out-of-body, to accomplish exploits in the earth. Furthermore, spirit travel in the earth has the potential to be very practical in nature, solving very real problems in answer to very real prayers. The chaplain was on his knees praying, presumably for deliverance, when at that moment the Lord stepped in and sent one of his servants to go and get him out, just like when the Lord sent an angel to rescue Peter out of prison in Acts 12. God is not always looking for the most qualified individual to do His work—He wants the willing because He qualifies those He has called.

In the following chapter we will take a look at how the Lord can sometimes call upon us to travel in the spirit during the night, when our minds are asleep but our spirits remain wide awake.

Chapter 7

Dreams and Dimensions

When we fall asleep our minds are resting, yet in spite of the dormancy of our consciousness, in REM sleep we can still have dreams. Not only do we dream, but they can be interpreted and have a practical and meaningful application in our physical lives. Sometimes we encounter information in our dreams that our conscious minds had no prior knowledge of before we fell asleep. I know a very minimal amount of Japanese, having studied only a basic level in high school, but recall one dream years ago where someone was speaking to me in that language. If I could have remembered what they said upon awakening, I could have looked it up and translated, but the fact remains that they were saying words I literally do not know and have never learned. Because I know a small amount of Japanese and have a knack for languages, I was able to recognize it the moment I heard it, but how did I manage to dream in words that I neither know nor understand? Where does this information come from? I believe it comes from our spirits. Just because our bodies sleep doesn't mean our spirits do. After all, they are not hindered by the constraints of the natural world to begin with, and sleep is a limitation placed only on our physical bodies. What is our spirit man supposed to do for the six to eight hours we spend asleep at night—twiddle its ethereal thumbs? Of course not, which is where traveling in the spirit comes in.

Sleep is a period that rejuvenates our bodies and minds, and in doing so it also releases our spirits to roam freely through the various dimensions of time and space—possibly even to experience aspects of eternity while our bodies lay dormant in this time-realm. I can recall brief snippets of dreams where I have talked to angels or had meaningful conversations with other people I know, only to forget everything we said upon waking, merely recalling that we were discussing deep and purposeful things. Everyone has at one time or other experienced *de ja vu*, a word that expresses the feeling we have done something before even though we are doing it physically for the first time. There is a simple explanation for this—sometime in the past while we were asleep our spirit man already experienced that future moment, which explains the sense of recognition and familiarity we get when we live out that event the second time around. Because our conscious minds were not aware of it, we think it is the first time we have encountered the event, but deep down we know and can feel that something is familiar—very familiar.

I believe the *Bible* gives us a little glimpse into how this process of remembering events that haven't happened before works. Job 33:14-16 (*NASB*) says, "Indeed God speaks once, or twice, yet no one notices it. 'In a dream, a vision of the night, when sound sleep falls on men, while they slumber in their beds, then He opens the ears of men, and seals their instruction . . .'" This passage explains that God gives us instructions in our sleep but *seals it up* for a future time. I have certain areas in life where I have instinctively known things to be true—such as in the late 2000s when teachings about Quantum Physics and the Prophetic were starting to emerge. For whatever reason, I would hear these teachings as a 25-year-old and be grossly unimpressed. Why? What they were saying wasn't wrong, but I found it boring to listen to, not to mention extremely obvious. The fact is that it really *wasn't* all that obvious—or it shouldn't have been. Somehow I already knew many of these things even though I had never had the information taught to me before. I believe that in my dreams God had sealed this information up in my spirit man, and as I had conversations with people on these subjects, the information rose to the surface without ever needing formal instruction. It still happens to me at times to this day—where stored understanding comes out at just the right time with no explanation for where I learned it. This is different from the word of knowledge or word of wisdom because I am familiar with those and both involve receiving revelation in a particular moment. This is information that is brought up from the depths within me that I can sense has been there for a while—I simply had been unaware of it in my conscious mind.

Gleaning sealed knowledge is by no means the only thing our spirits do while we slumber. I have had dreams before that I now recognize weren't actually dreams but were my spirit traveling about in the heavens and the earth while I was asleep. I have done it many times while awake on purpose, and there have been other times that I recall feeling that a dream seemed exceptionally more vivid or real upon waking than other dreams, but only two such ones can I specifically remember.

The first was in the early 2000s during the second Bush Administration's occupation of Afghanistan after the Trade Center Bombings on September 11, 2001. I was standing in the desert somewhere by a large rocky outcropping of some kind. There was a U.S. soldier there wearing light, sandy-colored camouflage with an automatic weapon of some sort. I can only imagine he must have been on some kind of patrol duty as it was completely dark out. He was alone, which I only realized long after the fact seems exceedingly strange when occupying a foreign land. Anyway, he and I had a short conversation, but all I remember of that conversation was telling him the following: "Both of my brothers have been to Afghanistan already, so I guess now it is my turn."

On waking this comment seemed particularly odd to me because at that time it was true that both of my brothers *had* been to Afghanistan via the military posting them there, and I thought the dream was a prophetic message telling me I needed to travel there for some unknown reason. It was only a number of years later that I realized that it hadn't been a dream at all—my spirit had taken a trip to Afghanistan to speak to a soldier while my body was asleep in my bed. I had told the soldier it was *my turn* to be in Afghanistan because I *was* in Afghanistan, right then when I thought I was dreaming.

I should mention here that it is possible to time-travel in the spirit realm as well, so time-of-day is not necessarily an indicator of veracity in travel. What I mean by way of example is that the Afghanistan trip took place at night while I was sleeping, but it was *also* at night for the soldier—which given we were on opposite sides of the world would have been impossible unless time travel of some kind was involved. On the other hand, this next encounter I had seemed to match up very accurately with real-time events.

The second nighttime traveling event I remember was much more recently—in the summer of 2015. I had worked the night before as a night-shift RN at a local hospital, so in the morning I laid down to sleep. I dreamed I was in the play-room on the pediatric oncology ward of a modern hospital. From what I could tell based on the details in the dream, I was somewhere in the United States and it was daytime. I followed a girl, probably eight to ten years old, into the play room. She was pulling her IV pole in tow and was upset because of something a boy there was saying about God or Jesus, but I do not recall what he said. She, however, was near tears.

I don't think I actually talked to her directly but turned my attention to some adults who were in the room. One was a male doctor of Asian descent who was somewhat tall with short black hair and wearing blue scrubs. There were two female nurses present, one of whom had long dark hair that was very curly. I did not get a good look at the second nurse, but I am pretty sure they were both RNs. I spoke to them about death and loss and informed that because I was also a nurse that I, too, have had patients die. I shared that I understood their difficulty in dealing with death and how they felt. I reassured them that I was not trying to make light of their feelings in any way, but that I did understand.

I then went on to remind them that what they were doing was God's work and that in reality, all they had to do was turn to God any and every time they were having difficulty and didn't feel like they could continue in their line of work. I exhorted them that God could take all of their sadness and grief and that what they needed was to stay close to Him to get inner healing for all their emotional hurts so they could continue moving forward to tend to the needs of these children. I reminded them they did need to tend to these children's needs and bring healing to them as well.

That was the end of what I recall of that experience, but it struck me upon waking that at least one of those three staff members must have been very close to quitting and needed to hear what I said to them. Turnover rates from staff on oncology units are high to begin with, and even higher in pediatric oncology. This is largely due to the emotional stress of regularly dealing with death, but in pediatric oncology there is a steady stream of young people dying, and working in places that have constant reminders of mortality and human suffering can be overwhelming to oncology staff. I was also struck by the fact that it was after 8:00 am in the morning on the West Coast of the United States when I had this dream, late enough that anywhere in the country at that time there would actually have been doctors and nurses awake and at work on day shift. In other words, the time of day I experienced in the dream correlated with the time of day it actually was outside the dream, which served in my mind as a further confirmation that I had indeed traveled in the spirit in my sleep. While the time of day can be misleading in these encounters, and therefore should not really be used to corroborate events, it is interesting nonetheless to consider that I had actually spoken with medical staff in another hospital elsewhere in the nation while lying asleep in my bed.

I found both of these experiences to be unique in that I do not now recall every detail or even why I was there at the time, nor did I receive some type of clear divine instruction in the encounters prior to being taken there. I simply appeared where I needed to be and it occurred while I was asleep. I do not know if I will ever meet the soldier, or the doctor and nurses, or that little girl, but I trust that whatever I did had lasting fruit and that God was responsible for orchestrating my spirit to travel throughout the earth where and when it was needed. In fact, in both instances I had some sort of connection to the event, which I believe was divinely designed to help the other people open up in some way to what I had to share. In the first case, I had a close family tie to the military and Afghanistan, which could have helped open the door with that soldier. In the second, I work in a hospital as a nurse so was able to show professional solidarity and in doing so gain access to speak to their hearts. While I cannot claim that one must always have some sort of *connection* to be invited by the Lord to spirit travel on a specific assignment, I do trust the Lord has a way of working those sorts of things out for everyone's highest good.

As we continue to pursue traveling in the spirit I believe we can expect these sorts of experiences will occur with greater frequency. I had another prophetic encounter once while awake where I had done something in the spirit, and afterwards the Lord asked me to choose between one of a few rewards. Of the spiritual items He offered me, I opted for a skill book, which in online role-play games is something that teaches the game character a new skill or ability that will stay with them and further develop as one plays. This might not speak to everyone, but having already published a book called *The Gamer's Guide to the Kingdom of God* at the time of this encounter, a book which outlined just these sorts of things, it was very meaningful to me. I was excited to discover upon opening the skill book that it was for engaging spirit travel in my sleep. While I had already done so prior to receiving this spiritual gift, I do remember that when I woke up the next morning, my dream had included some type of spirit-travel event. While regretfully I cannot recall the actual nature *of* the spirit travel encounter that night, I know that I did have one, and it was proof to me that this skill was active and that over time what the Lord had given me would continue to bear even more fruit.

Fragments In Our Dreams

In the past few years, I have been introduced to something known as *fragments*—fractured parts of the soul that are used to protect our core personality from emotional trauma. I will not go into great depth here as to the many particulars of fragmentation and fragment healing as this is not the focus of this book, but I will give a brief explanation and then discuss some revelation that pertains to traveling in the spirit. Before going further, let it be made clear that I am not a psychologist or psychiatrist and my existing medical credentials as a nurse do not cover diagnosis or treatment for people with any form of dissociative disorder or other related medical condition. Everything shared here is anecdotal and nothing in this book is a substitute for treatment under a licensed clinician, nor does purchasing or reading this material constitute as creating a client-practitioner relationship between the reader and me.

To briefly explain the theory of how these fragments or parts are formed, when we experience trauma our souls/minds/spirits break off little parts of themselves as a protective mechanism, hiding away the memories of painful events to allow us to function normally in spite of our brokenness. In order to become emotionally whole, we must both heal and integrate or reattach these broken pieces of the soul back to our core self. When we identify these fragmented parts, we can then seek healing in prayer to bring ourselves back to wholeness.

Whether one has experienced this in his life or not, I personally believe that every single person on the planet has at least one fragment that can be integrated back into the core self and that each of us would benefit from working through fragment integration. Some people have a diagnosed medical condition called Dissociative Identity Disorder (DID) of which the older term was Multiple Personality Disorder (MPD). Clinically speaking, people with DID have had their brain and/or soul break into multiple parts whether through traumatic events or chemical means. Studies have shown that certain life events, such as abuse at a young age (and harmful, highly traumatic events we don't always think of as abuse including routine male infant circumcision), are more likely to cause the brain to change how it develops, forming these alternate identities. Each part has some semblance of sentience and personality, sometimes even speaking different languages or having their own unique accent, gender, or age.

While I do not have a DID diagnosis, nor do I realistically even qualify medically for one, I have experienced some of my own fragments while working with a prayer counselors. Some parts have had a different age, accent, or gender, and while many of them have different names, some of them have no name at all. Since first becoming aware of them, I have had other profound healing encounters on my own without a prayer counselor present, and I have been able to use my skill with spirit travel to gain additional wholeness. I recently co-authored a book titled *Broken to Whole: Inner Healing for the Fragmented Soul* which is goes into much more depth on this subject for those interested in pursuing healing in this vital area. Traveling in the spirit, or at least the skill we use to engage it, is one of the means by which we can interact and work with these parts to bring inner healing to the soul.

In the same way that I have traveled in the spirit in my dreams, I have had dreams that involved these fragments. Furthermore, in my dreams these fragments were literally located in alternate dimensions. Interdimensional travel is currently impossible from a scientific perspective, but we are capable of traveling through space, time, and dimension by way of our spirits, so while this was a bit surprising at first, it makes much more sense when we consider our limitations have been removed in Christ Jesus.

I once had a series of fragment dreams all in the same night—the first time I guzzled a significant quantity of an ingredient in the flower essence called Fragment Finder developed by Freedom Flowers, designed to help reveal and integrate these various parts. At the time I was working in collaboration with Freedom Flowers, producing a line of gemstone essences from the heavenly gems we have received in the past (details are in my book *Gemstones From Heaven*). Not wanting to waste the leftover essence water, my wife and I each drank a considerable portion of it—probably multiple pints of water each in total. I should clarify that these are *not* essential oils, and *unlike* most essential oils, flower essences can and should be consumed internally—just not in the quantity that we did—unless one is prepared for some type of inner-healing crisis (for reference, one typically takes a few drops at a time). No crisis came to me that night, but I did have a series of extremely unique and insightful dreams, with each dream depicting one of my fragments either fighting forces of darkness or coming to terms with his reality and life experiences. While all of these dreams were very significant to me, one in particular stuck out as yielding new knowledge regarding the ability to cross dimensions in the spirit.

In this particular dream, I dreamt of a fragment who was very self-aware, but did not realize he was a fragment of mine. He viewed himself as his own person, not as a fractured part of someone else. The dream began with this fragment in an apartment at a gathering. The group of people present seemed like they were his youth group or other informal Christian home gathering. He was trying to let them know that he wasn't crazy, but then shared with them that he only had two weeks' worth of memories, and that something else strange was happening. He told the group he could sense he was sharing knowledge with another version of himself in another dimension. Because his memories were so limited, he recognized that logically he shouldn't know very much, but he knew basic scientific rules that he didn't remember learning in the two weeks prior—things like the expansion and contraction of matter based on temperature. He could literally sense the transmission of this information from his counterparts in other dimensions, and told as much to the group.

Upon waking from this dream, what I found fascinating is the interplay of possibilities suggested by this part. If this fragment had his own existence in another dimension, who was he talking to? Was this group of people he was talking to another set of fragments from other people? Or were they parts of mine as well, but they just didn't know it? Is it possible that this fragment was having a real-life existence in another very real dimension that has its own humans created by God, and upon integration, he will simply disappear from that realm entirely? And if he only had two weeks of memory, did I have some type of traumatic event two weeks prior that caused him to form? Considering I couldn't recall any, is it possible that time runs at an entirely different pace in his dimension compared to mine? There is no way to objectively know the answers to these questions, but it opens wide the door of possibilities of what *could* happen. When we travel in the spirit, can we liberate fragments held in these dimensions? Can we use this capacity to integrate our own parts or even set other people's fragments free and send them back to the core souls to whom they belong?

In my own life I have engaged some of my own parts in the spirit to work with and integrate them, but I find this possibility of other dimensions fascinating, and when we combine my dream-encounters with Hope's dimensional spirit travel as explained in the previous chapter, this subject starts to take on a deeper air of legitimacy. We already know the realms of the spirit are vast, but opening up alternate dimensions only widens that great expanse further. We know so little as of yet that I don't have a specific conclusion on this subject, but I believe we must realize there is much we have yet to learn. As we travel through the various spiritual spheres, we must remember to remain open to such possibilities since this is the kind of revelation that God will bring us as He helps us to grow and mature.

As a final note to this chapter, I believe that as we continue to pursue this ability to spirit travel, we will find ourselves remembering more and more of our time spent asleep. We will become able to activate this ability further and more in our slumber, and what will seem like lucid dreaming will actually be our spirits interacting in the heavens and the earth. Some have traveled in their dreams and woken with physical signs on their bodies, changes that would only be possible if their spirits had actually gone and done what they experienced in their dream and brought the effects back with them. I believe God desires for us to grow to a place where we can initiate these nighttime-experiences and travel to the places of greatest need in the earth, ministering to those who are in danger and need without ever leaving our homes and while fast asleep.

Chapter 8:

Consorting With The Dead

Traveling in the spirit opens up a realm of different questions and possibilities related to dead people. Can we visit our deceased loved ones? Isn't consorting with the dead forbidden in the *Bible*? What if I am praying to raise my loved one from the dead and they tell me in the spirit that they don't want to return? As we discover that we can indeed go into the heavens and communicate with those who are in the cloud of witnesses, these kinds of issues move from mere theory to reality. I will attempt to answer these questions as best as I can in this and the next chapter, looking at what the Scripture says and expanding on it further.

One of the fears some Christians have that is somewhat related to spirit travel has to do with consorting with the dead. As we travel into heaven itself, at some point we are likely to bump into someone we know who has died and gone to heaven, and if so, what do we do? After all, the *Bible* does tell us not to speak with the dead in multiple places:

- "Do not turn to mediums or necromancers; do not seek them out, and so make yourselves unclean by them: I am the Lord your God" (Leviticus 19:31).

- "If a person turns to mediums and necromancers, whoring after them, I will set my face against that person and will cut him off from among his people" (Leviticus 20:6).

- "A man or woman who is a medium or spiritist among you must be put to death. You are to stone them; their blood will be on their own heads" (Leviticus 20:27).

- "When you enter the land the Lord your God is giving you, do not learn to imitate the detestable ways of the nations there. Let no one be found among you who . . . is a medium or spiritist or who consults the dead." (Deuteronomy 18:9-11).

- "Saul died because he was unfaithful to the Lord; he did not keep the word of the Lord and even consulted a medium for guidance, and did not inquire of the Lord" (1 Chronicles 10:13-14a).

- "And when they say to you, 'Inquire of the mediums and the necromancers who chirp and mutter,' should not a people inquire of their God? Should they inquire of the dead on behalf of the living?" (Isaiah 8:19).

Consulting the dead is prohibited in the Old Testament, largely because God did not want the Israelites imitating the occult practices of the pagans who lived around them. Furthermore, God knew that the dead are not all-knowing. Certainly the deceased may have more insight about some things than we do because they have a different perspective, but death does not grant instant foreknowledge nor depth of insight into world events. One of the reasons spiritual growth is so important here on earth is that our beliefs on earth significantly influence what we are able to perceive in the spiritual realms after death. If someone has spiritual limitations on earth, they don't immediately reach enlightenment upon crossing over—it is a gradual process of revelation that alters their perspective slowly, even if that "slow" is fast compared to us here on earth. Their understanding is still veiled after death, and they still have to go through a process of removing those veils as they grow. This plays out when reading Near-Death Experiences as well, in that one's pre-death beliefs have a significant impact on one's experiences on the Other Side. In other words, asking your dead grandmother about something might yield an answer, but that answer could be just as inaccurate as it would have been if you had asked her something she knew nothing about while she was alive.

God also knows that we can be led astray by demons who are masquerading as our ancestors, and when we choose to seek answers in places where God does not approve, we open ourselves up to the consequences, which being misled is the least of such problems. If we feel the answers are useful then we are bound to continue to return, almost treating mediumship like a drug, coming back to get another hit again and again, addicted. Most people enjoy the supernatural to some extent or another because we know there is "more" out there, but there are wise and foolish ways to go about it. God has forbidden mediumship because He knows it can be harmful.

On the other hand, mediumship isn't necessarily inaccurate, nor is one guaranteed to speak with demons when consulting a medium. Take the example of King Saul when he consulted the witch of Endor. First Samuel 28:3-20 says:

> Now Samuel was dead, and all Israel had mourned for him and buried him in his own town of Ramah. Saul had expelled the mediums and spiritists from the land. The

Philistines assembled and came and set up camp at Shunem, while Saul gathered all Israel and set up camp at Gilboa. When Saul saw the Philistine army, he was afraid; terror filled his heart. He inquired of the Lord, but the Lord did not answer him by dreams or Urim or prophets. Saul then said to his attendants, "Find me a woman who is a medium, so I may go and inquire of her."

"There is one in Endor," they said.

So Saul disguised himself, putting on other clothes, and at night he and two men went to the woman. "Consult a spirit for me," he said, "and bring up for me the one I name."

But the woman said to him, "Surely you know what Saul has done. He has cut off the mediums and spiritists from the land. Why have you set a trap for my life to bring about my death?"

Saul swore to her by the Lord, "As surely as the Lord lives, you will not be punished for this."

Then the woman asked, "Whom shall I bring up for you?"

"Bring up Samuel," he said.

When the woman saw Samuel, she cried out at the top of her voice and said to Saul, "Why have you deceived me? You are Saul!"

The king said to her, "Don't be afraid. What do you see?"

The woman said, "I see a ghostly figure coming up out of the earth."

"What does he look like?" he asked.

"An old man wearing a robe is coming up," she said.

Then Saul knew it was Samuel, and he bowed down and prostrated himself with his face to the ground. Samuel said to Saul, "Why have you disturbed me by bringing me up?"

"I am in great distress," Saul said. "The Philistines are fighting against me, and God has departed from me. He no longer answers me, either by prophets or by dreams. So I have called on you to tell me what to do."

Samuel said, "Why do you consult me, now that the Lord has departed from you and become your enemy? The Lord has done what he predicted through me. The Lord has torn the kingdom out of your hands and given it to one of your neighbors—to David. Because you did not obey the Lord or carry out his fierce wrath against the Amalekites, the Lord has done this to you today. The Lord will deliver both Israel and you into the hands of the Philistines, and tomorrow you and your sons will be with me. The Lord will also give the army of Israel into the hands of the Philistines."

Immediately Saul fell full length on the ground, filled with fear because of Samuel's words. His strength was gone, for he had eaten nothing all that day and all that night.

When the witch called up Samuel's spirit, Samuel was successfully contacted and he did speak hidden knowledge from the other side. However, we must remember that Samuel was God's mouthpiece prior to his death which positioned him uniquely to have such foreknowledge as compared to most deceased spirits. This doesn't make what Saul did acceptable, but it does show us that it is possible to call up spirits of the dead into our physical realm. If we can call them to our realm then we certainly can connect with them in theirs through spirit travel. The question that remains then, is "should we?" The short answer is "that depends." The longer answer is a bit more involved.

Can we visit our deceased loved ones? If asking is it possible, the answer is yes. I have a friend whose sister died a number of years ago. I went with her to the hospital while the sister was still on life support and we prayed for healing, but after she died my friend traveled in the spirit to go find her, and she both found her and did speak with her. When people die their spirits do not dissipate—if we have the ability to interact in the spiritual spheres then we can communicate with them regardless of whether alive or dead in body.

Back in 2008 on Christmas Eve I was coming back home from work and stopped by our apartment in Palmyra, PA with a plan to head out shortly thereafter to meet my wife at a family member's house for the night. I was outside the building when I became aware of a presence near me. Honing in on what I was sensing, I realized it was my grandfather—my father's dad who died when I was in high school about seven years prior. I couldn't see him, but I could sense his presence, and somehow I clearly knew inside that it was him. At the time, this experience was at the very edge of my comfort zone, and I was wary and on guard. I asked Holy Spirit what I was supposed to do, but He just told me to listen to my grandfather, who shared a few details about my family and left. I had never sought him out prior and neither have I since—this was an encounter that happened to me without any effort or seeking on my part. When I got to my destination I was still pondering this and wasn't sure if I wanted to tell my wife because it was so off-the-wall even for us at the time, but I did tell her and she took it in stride.

What is my point in sharing all this? There is far more about the spiritual realms than we understand. God is not against us communicating with those who have died—He just doesn't want us to do it in wrong and unhealthy ways. How can I say that God isn't against us communicating with the dead when I just shared all of those *Bible* verses that condemn mediumship, necromancy, and consulting spiritists, all of whom had close contact with spirits of the dead? They don't tell the whole story.

Matthew 22:31b-32 says, ". . . have you not read what God said to you, 'I am the God of Abraham, and the God of Isaac, and the God of Jacob'? He is not God of the dead, but of the living." This means that according to Jesus, those who have died are not actually dead, really, but are alive elsewhere in nonphysical bodies—or at the very least those who are followers of God exist in that state. Hebrews 11:38-12:2 says this:

> These were all commended for their faith, yet none of them received what had been promised, since God had planned something better for us so that only together with us would they be made perfect. Therefore, since we are surrounded by such a great cloud of witnesses, let us throw off everything that hinders and the sin that so easily entangles. And let us run with perseverance the race marked out for us. . ."

If Jesus said they are alive then they are alive. If alive, then the prohibition about consorting with the dead doesn't apply, at least with them. Does this mean that we can talk to the dead so long as they were believers? You might look at it like that, but laying that down as a rule creates an equally problematic situation since no one but God knows the heart and it is impossible to know if a spirit is "saved." At the end of the day this is something each of us has to be individually led by the Holy Spirit about, but it does mean that those hard-and-clear prohibitions found in the Old Testament were made less-hard and less-clear by Jesus. Let us recall that Jesus himself spoke with some dead men (well, one of them) on the Mount of Transfiguration. Let us review that passage:

After six days Jesus took with him Peter, James and John the brother of James, and led them up a high mountain by themselves. There he was transfigured before them. His face shone like the sun, and his clothes became as white as the light. Just then there appeared before them Moses and Elijah, talking with Jesus.

Peter said to Jesus, "Lord, it is good for us to be here. If you wish, I will put up three shelters—one for you, one for Moses and one for Elijah."

While he was still speaking, a bright cloud covered them, and a voice from the cloud said, "This is my Son, whom I love; with him I am well pleased. Listen to him!" (Matthew 17: 1-5)

If we recall, Elijah ascended to heaven in a whirlwind while still alive, but Deuteronomy 34:5 states quite clearly that Moses died, which means Jesus was having a face-to-face conversation with a dead man and two verses later God declares from the heavens that He is pleased with Him! We are surrounded by a cloud of witnesses who are waiting for us to finish our portion of the relay race they began (Hebrews 12:1). They are cheering us on, and since the *Bible* says we are *surrounded* by them, it seems a bit unreasonable to expect that we wouldn't rub elbows with them now and again.

David Hogan publicly shared a story about an encounter he once had with his truck and a strange man he found inside it. Now understand, David Hogan has a wonderful heart, but he lives in the jungle with dangerous people and knows when not to joke around. When he walked out of where he was staying to find a stranger sitting in his truck, he was less than pleased. The man introduced himself as Isaiah, and stated he was sent by God to tell David to read his book—the book of Isaiah. As I recall, shortly after delivering this message, Isaiah disappeared. David didn't do anything to hunt down this dead prophet, nor did he invite Isaiah to hang out in his truck. Nevertheless this presumed-dead prophet was alive enough to appear in his truck, deliver him a message, and vanish again into the ethers.

We need to expand our understanding of what is permissible to us under the New Covenant based on the new revelation Jesus gave us about those who have gone before us being counted among the living, not the dead. In 1 Corinthians 6:12 Paul quoted and agreed with a common proverb of his day, stating that all things are permissible to us. And this is true. Yet, he further cautioned that while anything is allowed, not everything is beneficial, so it stands that we have to decide whether this practice is not just allowed, but a good idea. When the Scriptures show us that God is permissive in some area but does not directly command our involvement, this is decided on an individual basis—each person deciding in his or her heart what the Lord is leading him to do and walking that revelation out accordingly. An easy trap to fall into is the one where we start to treat our personal revelation on this somewhat subjective topic as law when God is simply opening the way before us without expectation of what we must or must not do in this regard. If someone does not feel they want to pursue communicating with the cloud of witnesses that is just as fine as if they believe this is a promise God has for them and want to move forward. In the following chapter, we will continue this discussion about speaking to spirits who have died, but we will look at it from a slightly different angle, discussing whether it is appropriate to consult them when praying to raise the dead.

Chapter 9

Raising The Dead

As the Founder of the Raise the Dead Initiative (RDI) and author of two books on resurrection, one of the most common questions I hear when teaching about raising the dead is "What if my loved one doesn't want to return?" This subject only becomes relevant if we believe it is possible to communicate with those who have crossed over to begin with, as discussed in the previous chapter. The Church of Jesus Christ is fairly unhealthy in our understanding of God's will for resurrection and life, and questions like this not only erode faith for resurrection, but they set themselves in opposition to God's nature which is always and ever after abundant life.

When we realize we have the ability to travel in the spirit and speak to those who have physically died, it becomes possible, at least at times, to ask their opinion of whether they want to return to the earth or not. At first glance, this sounds like a great idea and a wonderful opportunity that has been set before us, but as with all things we have to discern not only what spirit we are engaging, but the will of the Lord in the situation. Consulting the dead to see if they want to return or not ignores the most basic facts about Jesus's death and resurrection, not to mention God's overall will and plan for humanity and the commands He has given us. While we do have the ability to speak to the cloud of witnesses, seeking opinions from dead people about resurrection, even from the person we are trying to raise, is an inappropriate and genuinely terrible use of this ability.

There are multiple problems with this idea that might not be plainly obvious, so I will do my best to spell it out here. Keep in mind that my book *Faith to Raise the Dead* is designed to delve much more deeply into the theology surrounding dead-raising, so if this topic interests you or if you have questions that are not covered here, I recommend you get that book and read it, as this single chapter is insufficient to cover everything one might want to know, and I go into much more depth on this and related topics.

Resurrection begins with an understanding that our Heavenly Father is 100% anti-death. 1 Corinthians 15:26 says it quite plainly, "The last enemy to be destroyed is death." The Scriptures also tell us that eventually everyone is going to get resurrected anyway and no one will be permitted to remain dead. Jesus said such to Martha in John 11:21-26:

> "Lord," Martha said to Jesus, "if you had been here, my brother would not have died. But I know that even now God will give you whatever you ask."
>
> Jesus said to her, "Your brother will rise again."
>
> Martha answered, "I know he will rise again in the resurrection at the last day."
>
> Jesus said to her, "I am the resurrection and the life. The one who believes in me will live, even though they die; and whoever lives by believing in me will never die. Do you believe this?"

Martha was familiar with the last-day resurrection, and at no time did Jesus contradict her. He simply revealed a deeper truth—that there is a now-resurrection available. Paul discussed this truth about a last-day resurrection in 1 Corinthians 15:51-52 when he said, "Listen, I tell you a mystery: We will not all sleep, but we will all be changed—in a flash, in the twinkling of an eye, at the last trumpet. For the trumpet will sound, the dead will be raised imperishable, and we will be changed." Scripturally speaking, there are zero people who God will permit to remain dead in the long run—so honoring what we perceive a dead person's will to be is actually just going to be a short term thing—it won't last! Paul said again in 1 Corinthians 15:20, "But in fact, Christ has been raised from the dead. He is the first of a great harvest of all who have died." Jesus is our example and is the first fruits of *all who have died*. Our example and the person whose image we are to be conformed into is of a Jesus who was resurrected, not one who remained dead.

Regarding who to raise and who not to, there are various factors to consider, such as time and ability to pray to begin with, but the one thing that is *never* a factor we should consider is the will of the deceased regarding whether they want to return or not. Remember that even in a court of law, the will of the dead is largely irrelevant unless a legal document is produced, signed in advance by the deceased while they were still alive. The court doesn't call in a local prophet or spiritist to consult the spirit of the dead. If no prior wishes were legally ratified, then it is left up to those who are left behind—those of us who are there to pray and bring them back. When we lose our body, we lose the right to make decisions in the earth. Furthermore, our job here isn't as heavenly court-ordered will-adjudicators, but as heirs of God whose job it is to reverse and destroy the power of death.

I do not see a single place in the life of Jesus, much less the entire *Bible* where it suggests, demonstrates, or alludes to the idea that we should inquire of the will of the dead before praying to raise them. On the contrary, in Matthew 10:7-8 Jesus instructed his disciples to go all throughout the nation of Israel healing the sick and raising the dead. He didn't give them advance instructions about which ones wanted to stay in heaven. He didn't tell them to go interview the spirits of the deceased to make sure they wanted to come back. Jesus kept it really simple—if they were dead, bring them back to life because He *is* life.

Jesus made His will and position clear in John 10:10 where he said, "The thief comes only to steal and kill and destroy; I have come that they may have life, and have it to the full." He outlined Satan's purpose clearly—as the one who seeks death, loss, and destruction, but contrasted that by stating that He, Jesus, came to give us life. If death is Satan's goal and life is Jesus' will for us, if we choose not to raise the dead we are literally setting ourselves in opposition to God and working as servants of Satan in that matter.

Even as Paul said it, a great harvest of everyone who has died isn't a suggestion that one or two should get raised, but that it is God's will for everyone to return. What that means to me is that any deceased spirit who asks me not to bring them back is actually outside the will of God as stated in Scripture. As believers we are to submit to His will over ours and therefore the will of the dead seems entirely irrelevant to me. We know the will of our Father in Heaven, so I see no reason to ask permission of the dead to raise them, preferring instead to follow the commands of Jesus Christ.

The Lord spoke to me once and said, "No one who comes and experiences the glory of heaven wants to return to life on earth." It seems pretty sensible to me—after all, who wouldn't want Paradise over the pain, loss, and heartache available on the earth? The truth is that our job is to bring heaven to earth, not leave earth and escape to heaven. As we go on to maturity in spirit travel, we must understand this.

Let's be honest—Jesus was and is God of the Universe, and He was led by the Spirit in all he did while he was here on earth. I don't find it coincidental that even after he rose again He remained on the earth for another forty days spending time with his disciples. Yet neither prior to his death nor after his resurrection is it ever recorded that he gave the disciples instructions on how to discern the will of the dead. Truth be told, he didn't really address the subject at all, although Paul and some of the Old Testament prophets did. It wasn't like He was unaware of this ability to communicate with those who have died. Sometimes silence on a subject can be read as permission because there is nothing to negate it, and usually that is true. If God does not prohibit something and it aligns with his nature, then it is fair game in my mind, but discerning the will of the dead prior to praying to resurrect them is not one of those things because God's nature and his commands clearly contradict this idea.

To push this concept a little further, we have to remember that even Near Death Experiences (NDEs) often include God ignoring the will of the deceased. I have read countless firsthand reports where someone dies, goes to heaven, and then God either *asks* them to return to earth or He simply tells them they *may not remain in heaven* and *must* return. God seems to be in the habit of making His will known even to the dead—His desire is for them to return. And while yes, the argument could be made that the vast majority who remain dead *must* be those who chose to stay, not only do we have no actual data to prove that, we can know with certainty that is not always the case. Sometimes the dead are not raised due to demonic resistance, lack of faith, or a variety of other factors that have nothing to do with God's will in the situation. In fact, some people with NDE testimonies who almost *didn't* return have explained that demons were blocking re-entry into their bodies.

There are those who read this and hear me saying we should ignore the will of the dead and they get upset. Well, the reason it doesn't bother me is because I find God preferring to ignore their will too, and when even in NDEs the God of the Universe tells the dead they *must* return to life against their desires, I am not going to lose a lot of sleep over ignoring their will too; God clearly backs me on this. If I am able to bring the dead back to life in obedience to God, they can argue with Him later about their desire for Him to respect their free will, but that's not the job I have been given, and neither is it your job as a follower of Jesus Christ. Our task is to place death under His feet, not permit it to have room in our lives and the lives of those around us.

Has anyone ever considered how impractical and completely unrealistic it is to seek the will of the dead on this matter? The world often does a better job at pushing for life than we in the Church do. Pretend someone dies of a heart attack, or in a car accident, or a patient dies at the hospital where I work as a nurse. Do I hold off from doing CPR and push everyone else out of the room because we haven't properly ascertained the will of the dead before raising them? Do I sit down and get quiet and travel to them in the spirit for a quick conversation before starting chest compressions? No! From a medical perspective, whenever we are unclear about someone's legal status regarding resuscitation, we revive now and ask questions later.

There is no "good time" during a resurrection attempt to travel to the heavens and ask someone whether they want to come back or not. And the moment that we tell people that their loved one doesn't want to return, it destroys the faith they are engaging to stand for resurrection. I have seen this happen frequently—to the point that I had to ban people from sharing that revelation with one another in the Raise The Dead Initiative. I am not big on making rules, but the group is meant to be a safe and encouraging place for people to pursue raising their loved ones, and telling a praying family member that we got a revelation that their dead relative wants to stay dead, or worse yet, that God wants them dead, is entirely unacceptable. Yet some people still have the gall to tell a grieving widow who is standing on the promises of God in Scripture for her husband to return to life that God wants her husband, the father of her children, to stay dead. The group is about resurrection, not about faith-destroying for the sake of being *right*—in which case I would argue they only *think* they are right anyway. If someone wants to share that information and prophetic discouragement privately I cannot stop them, but I do not permit nor make room for that kind of demonic obstacle in my organization.

Next, we have to remember one key thing about spirit travel. It, along with all other prophetic interaction, is subject to being tested. We are all humans and every single one of us is fallible. I have a pretty good track record of prophetic accuracy, but even then I miss it from time to time. How can we even know for sure that we have heard correctly when we say that our loved one has told us they don't want to return? Even if we think we have heard God tell us the same, how can we be sure? As already explained, the Scriptures show us that we are always supposed to pray for life—so if we test that revelation against the *Bible* it will fail each and every time! Even 1 Kings 22:22 and 2 Chronicles 18:21 show us that an entire group of people can fall victim to a spirit of delusion, so other people confirming that person does indeed want to remain dead isn't even a sure-fire thing.

This is one of the key limitations of traveling in the spirit. We are allowed to do anything, but some things simply have no value or benefit to them (1 Corinthians 6:12)—and this is one of them. There are a number of things spirit travel is good for, but going into the heavens to inquire of the will of the dead regarding resurrection is one of the few times that speaking to the cloud of witnesses is entirely useless.

I recognize that this subject may seem a bit off-topic for some, but from my position as someone who trains people to raise the dead, this is an important aspect of spirit travel that the Body of Christ needs to hear. I believe it is a vital part of the discussion we must have as we pursue deeper levels of maturity in this area. In the following chapters, we will look at one of the reasons traveling in the spirit is essential to our spiritual walk—to engage in warfare against powers of darkness.

Chapter 10

Dealing With Powers of Darkness

One of the things that happen when we begin to delve into the realms of the spirit is that we discover the depths to which powers of darkness have been toiling in the earth. Witches, warlocks, and others who serve Satan and his underlings are already hard at work in the spiritual realms, and astral projection is not a new reality to them—it's simply part of regular life. I have not only read stories of such things happening but have had my own personal encounters with these servants of darkness. It is important to be aware of what our spiritual forays will involve us in, and how we will have to engage the enemy on a higher and more involved level than before. Shunning spirit travel will do nothing to reduce the size of the spiritual targets on our backs, and will simply render us less-aware of the battle already waged around us, making us less effective in it. In this case, ignorance is folly, not bliss.

I grew up learning about spiritual warfare. My parents were diligent to teach my brothers and me how to pray against demons and call in angelic protection to surround us, but dealing with powers of witchcraft was not included in my childhood training. I don't blame my parents for this—I can only presume it was their own lack of experience that created this gap. In late 2006 and early 2007, this knowledge deficit was remedied through a crash course in "Protection Against the Dark Arts" when my now-wife, I, and a few others were thrust into the middle of a spiritual battle I personally believe we were collectively unprepared to wage. We learned on our feet and the first battles were our victory, but due to oversight and inexperience on the part of some group members, we took a serious hit in the long run. I will share those lessons and events with you here.

That first encounter involved my wife, me, and a few others getting together for dinner, after which we ended up in a spiritual scuffle with the guy across the street and his girlfriend. After another student and I got back to the dorm and I was lying in bed, I realized the guy had followed us home—his astral body was three stories up outside and trying to get in the building. In order to address the problem I ended up waking up and angering the other student's roommate, and apparently even after I thought we dealt with it then, the other student had to lay awake the rest of the night still in warfare.

We all got together a few more times for fellowship. One such evening we were worshiping in my wife's living room, and in the spirit, I saw someone walking up the stairs to her second floor. It took me a moment to realize I was observing someone who had astral-projected into the house, but moments later I sprang into action. Sunshine and I walked upstairs as the others continued to worship and pray below. At the top of the stairs I turned left into the first bedroom, which had a doorway on the far end connecting to a bathroom and another small room.

Stepping into the room I immediately saw this person's astral form again, so I reached out and flung them across to the far wall. While this might sound strange to some, astral bodies rarely can interact with physical objects, but nothing is stopping me, a spirit being who lives in a body, from interacting with them. Thus, I threw him. He fell, and I watched him crawl on his hands and knees through the hallway into the other room; we followed. Upon entering that space, I saw a vision of four people standing there, all of whom had projected in. We summarily ejected them from the premises. It turned out we were battling an entire coven.

That night and the days that followed were an intense time of training, as I had never dealt with anything of this level before, and for the most part hadn't again until this past year. I discovered just how much our will directs what happens in the spirit realm. I discovered that there were prophets and prophetic people in ministry who were both aware of and able to spirit travel at will, but at that time were hiding it from the Body of Christ. I also discovered what happens when you win a battle but lose a war.

The next few years after this event, I found my energy for Christian activities drained away. I still loved God but I just didn't have any emotional reserve available to actually get involved in anything spiritual. During this time I read a number of books by a range of spiritual authors, some of whom lacked the revelation of Jesus Christ but have done fascinating and informative studies into a number of aspects of prayer, faith, miracles, and more. I didn't understand why I felt so spiritually drained until I read a book by shamanic teacher Ted Andrews titled *The Intercession of Spirits*. In this book, he discussed many things, but one chapter in particular spoke to me—he shared how at one point he saw himself as a "psychic white knight" and took on a guy who was spiritually harassing a friend. What Ted didn't know at the time was that this guy had an entire cult backing him, whereas Ted was alone. The moment I read this, a light bulb went on and I realized what I was experiencing was the result of fighting against a coven in a spiritual battle without fully understanding what I had been involved in.

This is the sort of thing that I find seldom discussed, but it would have been extremely helpful to have learned. It isn't something anyone I knew could have taught me simply because no one I knew had any experience in this arena to be able to teach—whether regarding spirit travel and astral projection, battling witches in the spirit, or anything else related. Since then I have found myself among others who have had a similar learning curve as myself—difficult but highly educational. I learned that what we oftentimes see as a one-time battle, they tend to view as a long-term war. When we think we are finished, they're just getting started. We have to be in it for the long-haul.

More recently, I have been in intercession for a friend who does a lot of work with inner healing and deliverance, and this individual was doing a lot of really intense prayer work that inadvertently aroused the ire of *many* covens simultaneously. For reasons I won't go into, the situation required much prayer, and it also involved a lot of ongoing spiritual warfare including dealing with many people astral projecting, among other things.

One night my wife and I stayed up late, along with intercessors around the North American continent, to pray into a particularly dicey problem this friend was dealing with. We had been fighting against a satanic high priest who had multiples of covens of witches backing him up in prayer, and he had created a spiritual barrier that we had to break through before we could accomplish the assignment before us. We were dealing with covens astral projecting on our property as were the other intercessors where they were located. After praying for hours my wife went to bed at 2 am but because the

Lord had specifically instructed me to stay awake until 4, I remained in prayer. And around 3:45 with only four of us left awake on this prayer team spanning the nation, we got the breakthrough. I had a vision at that time of a portal—a golden pillar of light that appeared in my living room. An arm thrust out of the portal with a piece of paper, which in the spirit I took and read. It said, "You're dead." I confess I was very confused by this event. In my experience golden portals are not usually from the enemy, but I don't take kindly to spiritual death threats either.

As I began to pray into what I was seeing, asking Holy Spirit to show me what was going on, I got a text from my deliverance minister friend who notified me they had broken the shield and finished the task. As confusing as it was, it seems the "You're dead" was not directed *at* me—instead it was a very confusing way to communicate the state of the high priest we were fighting against. I called my friend and told him what had just happened to me, and he began to laugh. What I saw was a confirmation to them, as well as quite funny considering what we had been dealing with (I'll be honest, I still don't understand why the revelation came through that way—it really was strange). I cannot say one way or the other whether the high priest in question actually died or not, as I have no idea where in the world this man was located, but I know we won that battle.

A key difference between the first set of witch-encounters and the latter set, which were almost ten years to the date, were two key things: perseverance and numbers. The first time we had mistakenly thought the battle was over when it was just getting started and paid the price. The second time around we continued to pursue the victory in prayer long after the initial battles had been won. During the first encounter, there were four of us whereas with the latter encounter (which at the time of writing, this is still an ongoing prayer issue) there are many more.

While it would be nice to say that quantity doesn't matter, there is a point in time where it does. As mentioned above, in the former battle there were four of us, but it was only against a single coven. In the latter there were dozens of us, but possibly even hundreds of covens. Deuteronomy 32:30 says, "How could one man chase a thousand, or two put ten thousand to flight, unless their Rock had sold them, unless the LORD had given them up?" Doing simple math here, if one can put a thousand to flight, what happens when you have one person but four thousand enemies? What happens if you have two people but only three thousand attackers? At some point in time the numbers do matter. Greater are they who are for us than those against us, which is why a few of us can win against a horde of powers of darkness, but at some point math still comes into play. If we lack total manpower to overcome the opposition, we are likely to eventually lose. Even if we have numbers on our side but we lack perseverance to stay strong in the battle, we can lose by attrition over time. Even a steady dripping of a tiny stream of water can wear away at a boulder if given long enough. This is why Paul exhorted the Ephesians so strongly in Ephesians 6:10-13:

> Finally, be strong in the Lord and in his mighty power. Put on the full armor of God, so that you can take your stand against the devil's schemes. For our struggle is not against flesh and blood, but against the rulers, against the authorities, against the powers of this dark world and against the spiritual forces of evil in the heavenly realms. Therefore put on the full armor of God, so that when the day of evil comes, you may be able to stand your ground, and after you have done everything, to stand.

We are exhorted to stand because there are times when we have done everything we can and the only solution is to continue to pray, continue to battle, and continue to press through. When we were fighting the high priest that was about all we could do. We had run out of every unique and interesting prayer by about eleven o'clock, but it took until almost four a.m. to finish the fight. What did we do in the five hours between eleven and four? We stood firm, praying in the spirit and continuing to battle unyieldingly. At those times there really isn't much else one can do other than persevere.

Spirit travel is not all rainbows, unicorns, and roses. There are other entities out there, some human and others not, some of whom serve powers of darkness and who seek our demise. They will seek to ensnare or delay us in the spiritual realms. The angel which Daniel 10 speaks of was not delayed in delivering his message to Daniel by heavy highway traffic, a long checkout line at the grocery store, or waiting for a babysitter to come watch the kids. Daniel 10:12-13 says:

> Then he continued, "Do not be afraid, Daniel. Since the first day that you set your mind to gain understanding and to humble yourself before your God, your words were heard, and I have come in response to them. But the prince of the Persian kingdom resisted me twenty-one days. Then Michael, one of the chief princes, came to help me, because I was detained there with the king of Persia."

A demon lord directly opposed the messenger in the spiritual realms, barring his way until Michael the Archangel came and cleared a path by keeping this dark Prince occupied in battle. If an angel sent from heaven can have his path obstructed, we are not immune to such issues. I remember hearing a testimony, mentioned in the preface, which revivalist Todd Bentley shared publicly. He was ascending in the spirit and the figure of an Eastern Monk appeared in front of him. This monk, or other spirit being appearing in that form, prevented him from ascending into the heavens and that particular encounter fell flat.

In his article titled *How Satan Stops our Prayers: Combat in the Heavenly Realms* John Mulinde shares a story he heard directly from the mouth of a man who had been raised to serve Lucifer. This man began to display powers at age four, was raised by witches after age six, and by age ten was actively at war against the churches of God. By the time he reached his twenties, he had committed many evil deeds, and his supernatural abilities surpassed most. As the story goes, one day he was assigned to destroy a church that was filled with prayer:

> There had been much division in this church, and much confusion. He began to work against it, but at that time, the pastor called a fast for the whole church. As the church began to fast, there was much repentance and a lot of reconciliation. The people came together and began to pray for the Lord to work in their midst. They continued interceding and crying out to God to have mercy on them and to intervene in their lives. As the days went by, the man came again and again against the church with demon spirits. But a word of prophecy came forth telling the Christians to rise up and wage warfare against the powers of darkness that were attacking the church.
>
> So one day, the man left his body in his room to go astro-travelling. He led a powerful force of demonic spirits against the church. Now this is his testimony: His spirit moved through the air over the church and tried to attack it, but there was a covering of light over the church. Suddenly, an

army of angels attacked them and fought against them in the air. All the demons fled, but he was arrested by the angels.

Yes, arrested by the angels! He found himself being held by about six angels. They brought him through the roof right before the church altar. He just appeared there as the people were praying. They were deep in prayer, engaged in spiritual warfare, binding and breaking and casting out. The pastor was on the platform leading the prayers and the warfare. The Spirit of the Lord spoke to the pastor, "The yoke has been broken, and the victim is there before you. Help him through deliverance." As the pastor opened his eyes, he saw the young man lying there. His body was with him; he was in his body. The young man said that he doesn't know how his body joined him; he had left it back in his house. But there he was in his body. He didn't know how he had entered it; all he knew was that the angel had carried him through the roof. (Mulinde)

This is yet another example of the goings-on in the spiritual realms. We are in a war, and the enemy plays for keeps. While we will not encounter the enemy every time we go traveling in the spirit, there are times that we will and we must have our eyes opened further to see the battles around us. 2 Corinthians 2:10-11 says, "Anyone you forgive, I also forgive. And what I have forgiven—if there was anything to forgive—I have forgiven in the sight of Christ for your sake, in order that Satan might not outwit us. For we are not unaware of his schemes." Forgiveness is a major weapon against powers of darkness and because we are aware of the schemes of the enemy, we cannot afford to hold things against one another. The above testimony shows us that unforgiveness is a tool the enemy uses to try to divide and destroy us, but when we come together in unity and prayer, we will rout the forces of evil.

So how, then, do we fight in the spirit? What are our weapons of warfare? First, as said above, forgiveness. We must cleanse ourselves of all agreement with darkness, letting ourselves be washed by the blood of Jesus and purified in His refining fire. Sometimes I will literally envision myself being washed in His blood with His cleansing fire purging everything negative or unholy out of me. As I do this, Holy Spirit may bring things to mind that I need to pray through or repent for, people to forgive, or even inner healing and deliverance needs, at which point I will address whatever comes up, even casting demons out of myself.

When I ascend in the spirit and do battle, I tend to envision a celestial battlefield, complete with whatever demons, witches, or other opponents are present. Usually, angels accompany me and we fight with swords, shields, and other weapons, as well as energy. It is hard to describe what fighting with energy looks like, but it is a bit like one might imagine if you had mutant powers and could fight by shooting light beams at the enemy. This method largely involves overwhelming the enemy by power and is not always effective in the short-term, but given long enough, as suggested above, it usually will eventually work.

I have had situations where I found myself casting a ruling spirit down, vacating a region in the spirit realm. Keep in mind that the spiritual world is far more vast than our earth, and there are territories beyond territories that are controlled by the powers of light and/or hordes of darkness. When I have been able to liberate any part of the spiritual spheres, I usually do a few things. First, I have the angels collect the spoils of war—spiritual weapons and other such belongings that the enemy has had to give up due to their loss. Second, I figure out how to establish Kingdom rule in the enemy's place—usually setting an angel in a position of rulership over that region or asking the Lord to do the same. Nature abhors a vacuum, and if we are going to create one in the spiritual realms by removing a demonic authority, we would be wise to replace it. This principle is found in Matthew 12:43-45 and repeated in Luke 11:24-26—when an area is vacated, if nothing fills the space then the enemy will reoccupy it and further fortify the region. Third, I look to see what to do with the plunder. The riches of the enemy have come as a result of their piracy—stealing from the people of God and from His angels as they carry answers from heaven to us here on earth. When I take over I commandeer those riches and release angels to either send them to their proper owner or if the matter has long-passed then I have them add it to my own spiritual wealth to be used later.

Spiritual warfare in this manner can be dicey, and if we engage in battles where we are overpowered and are unable to break through, we will lose. Because our spirit travel encounters have potential to make a positive impact on the natural world, it stands to reason that losing spiritual battles will have untold negative consequences on our lives as well.

While this is not a glamourous chapter, I believe it is important that we understand that not only is there a real spiritual battle with demonic forces, but there are humans who have willingly aligned themselves with powers of darkness and who actively seek out people to attack. Over the years I have removed spiritual seals, broken curses, and in other ways dealt with the influence of witchcraft attacks both over myself, my wife, and friends and family. This isn't a problem that goes away when we ignore it, and we must learn to become aware of the schemes of the enemy. We fight with powerful spiritual weaponry that is able to destroy the works of darkness and release the light of the Kingdom of God into the world. I have read the end of the book: Jesus wins. No matter how difficult or dark things may get, keep fighting, keep your head up, and continue to pursue Heaven–for greater is He who is in us than he who is in the world.

There is, however, another option when engaging in spirit-wars—to remove it from the battlefield entirely, opting to fight with authority instead of power. This next chapter will explain more about that method of warfare.

Chapter 11

The Courts of Heaven

The term *Courts of Heaven* refers to a series of teachings and beliefs about how to administrate God's justice in the earth by traveling in the spirit into courtrooms in the heavens. It has become increasingly popular over the past number of years, largely because of its effectiveness, especially when dealing with spiritual warfare or persistent problems that have not been adequately addressed through other methods of prayer. The Courts work because they enlist spiritual assistance by means of authority as opposed to the majority of spiritual battles which seem to be fought through power. Both power and authority have their upsides and downsides, but when one lacks sufficient power to get the job done as is often the case with persistent unresolved issues, turning to a different method is not only sensible, it has a better chance of being effective. This is where the Courts of Heaven come into play.

Before going further I should note that the entire process of engaging the Courts of Heaven involves spirit travel. Just the fact that we are going into the heavens in the spirit to do anything makes it, by definition, traveling in the spirit. Thus, while this chapter focuses on the Courts and the process involved and does not specifically address much regarding spirit travel, this is because the *entire process* involves spirit travel.

When I first came across this teaching years ago, a friend recommended a series of YouTube videos by Robert Henderson, a preacher and *Bible* teacher. Another article I found helpful was one titled *The Courts of Heaven* written by Jim Wies, coeditor of XP Publishing in October 2013. Years before that, I had been subscribed to *The ElijahList*, an internet publication of various articles from mainly charismatic Christian authors, teachers, and speakers, and came across one by Paul Cox from February 20th in 2006, titled *Heavenly Court*. While there are many good teachings out there on the subject, those three will give the reader a good background if interested in further research on this subject.

Having developed my own understanding of the Courts in the years that followed, I will give the simplest yet most thorough explanation I can of the scriptural basis behind this practice before we move on to the practical how-to of this system. In Courts of Heaven theory, intercession is best done in a courtroom, not a battlefield. Since Hebrews 4:16 points out that we have free access to come boldly before God's throne, this is a legitimate option given to us. What we need to remember is that God's kingdom is a benevolent monarchy, and God, as the King of Kings and Lord of Lords, is the highest authority in the land. While even current day monarchies have judicial systems, way back when, many legal matters were decided by the King. One prime scriptural example of this was Solomon presiding over matters of judgment in 1 Kings 3:16-28. Because our King is the head of the Heavenly Courts, we can seek audience with Him at any time to resolve spiritual conflicts with the enemy.

Jesus often spoke in parables, but in Luke 18:1-8 he explained prayer not as a form of spiritual warfare but from a perspective of using a legal system, which gives the Court Theory precedence:

> Then Jesus told his disciples a parable to show them that they should always pray and not give up. He said: "In a certain town there was a judge who neither feared God nor cared what people thought. And there was a widow in that town who kept coming to him with the plea, 'Grant me justice against my adversary.'
>
> "For some time he refused. But finally he said to himself, 'Even though I don't fear God or care what people think, yet because this widow keeps bothering me, I will see that she gets justice, so that she won't eventually come and attack me!'"
>
> And the Lord said, "Listen to what the unjust judge says. And will not God bring about justice for his chosen ones, who cry out to him day and night? Will he keep putting them off? I tell you, he will see that they get justice, and quickly. However, when the Son of Man comes, will he find faith on the earth?"

Jesus was very clear in this parable that it was a judicial ruling that got the job done, and he *immediately* went on to explain that God will bring people justice quickly—all in the context of the judicial system. If we look at those verses about prayer and think that it means we just need to pray harder to irritate God into action, we have missed the message. God is a just judge, but Jesus was making the point that if an unjust judge will do the right thing after sufficient pestering, how much more will a righteous judge bring justice on our behalf when we lodge a legal complaint? Remember here that the parable was talking about a widow. She didn't have a sword or other weapon and she wasn't out there attacking and attempting to overpower her enemy. In fact, she didn't address the enemy *at all*.

Revelation 12:10 tells us that we have an accuser of the brethren that accuses us before God day and night, and that we overcome through the blood of Jesus, the word of our testimony, and when we do not shrink back from death. Satan constantly accuses us before God because he wants to find every opportunity possible to tear us down. And while I am not a big fan of most of the teachings people derive from the first part of Job, Chapter 1:6 shows that Satan has some means of accessing the courts of heaven to speak against us before God. This same sentiment is echoed in Zechariah 3:1-4 which says:

> Then he showed me Joshua the high priest standing before the angel of the Lord, and Satan standing at his right side to accuse him. The Lord said to Satan, "The Lord rebuke you, Satan! The Lord, who has chosen Jerusalem, rebuke you! Is not this man a burning stick snatched from the fire?"
>
> Now Joshua was dressed in filthy clothes as he stood before the angel. The angel said to those who were standing before him, "Take off his filthy clothes." Then he said to Joshua, "See, I have taken away your sin, and I will put fine garments on you."

In this passage we see Satan standing in the heavens before God, accusing the High Priest Joshua. As a side note I have to say that I am not entirely sure how Satan can be accusing us before the throne when Revelation 12:9 clearly states, "The great dragon was hurled down—that ancient serpent called the devil, or Satan, who leads the whole world astray. He was hurled to the earth, and his angels with him." Nevertheless, between verses in Job 1, Zechariah 3, Revelation 12, 1 Peter 5, and others it seems clear that Satan has some measure of access to accuse us before God. In this verse in Zechariah, Jesus immediately flips the deal on Satan's head anyway, washing away Joshua's sin—symbolized by removing his filthy rags of sin and clothing him in garments of righteousness. Isaiah 61:10 echoes this, saying, "For he has clothed me with garments of salvation and arrayed me in a robe of his righteousness."

Jesus' blood is the single most powerful thing in our favor because it *removes the record of sin* that the enemy holds against us. Hebrews 1:3b says, "After he had provided purification for sins, he sat down at the right hand of the Majesty in heaven." Purification for our sins comes through Jesus' blood, and "He sat down" represents that Jesus did it once for all time and He doesn't have to do it anymore. Satan no longer has a legal means by which to bring suit against us, but that doesn't stop him from accusing us anyway. So what does Jesus do about it? Hebrews 7:25 says, "Therefore he is able to save completely those who come to God through him because he always lives to intercede for them." Jesus constantly intercedes for us. He is the primary advocate on our behalf in the Court System of Heaven; His testimony trumps everyone else's. In reality, His is the first and last testimony needed because once Jesus testifies, every accusation set against us is nullified.

The Scriptures reveal a judicial system in heaven that moves things beyond the scope of a battlefield and instead makes use of a legal system to bring about justice. Imagine a real-life situation where your neighborhood has been overrun by a violent gang, where nightly shootouts and murders are increasing. The neighborhood has become a battlefield. You have reached the point where hunkering down inside your house is no longer an option—especially since a number of your windows have already been shot out by bullets, and one such projectile narrowly missed your daughter's head while you were seated peacefully at the dinner table. Your choices are either to go into battle and take on the gang violence by yourself (and hope you don't die in the process) *or* avoid the battlefield entirely and go through the legal system, obtaining a judicial ruling to end the reign of terror once and for all. After going through the court system and having secured the legal decision, it sets events into motion that culminate in a final victory. In a single nighttime raid, the police round up every single gang member from both gangs and haul them off to jail, impound their assets, drain their bank accounts, and permanently dismantle both organizations. This is the earthly equivalent of what going through the Courts of Heaven can accomplish under the right circumstances.

I don't want to mislead you into thinking that the Courts are the panacea to fix all harms and right all wrongs because they don't and won't. As the saying goes, if the only tool you have is a hammer, then every problem must become a nail. It is not the best solution for every problem, but it can be very effective for certain issues. I have friends who regularly do inner healing and deliverance with victims of Satanic Ritual Abuse (SRA), and when up against high level witchcraft, the Courts of Heaven method is sometimes the only means for breakthrough because in some moments, nothing else works.

In order to put this teaching into action, most people use what are referred to as a set of protocols for operating in the courtrooms. This basically is just a set of rules or regulations on how things are done. These protocols can be extremely limiting regulations or a set of freeing guidelines; it all depends on who you talk to and how they use them. Protocols are common in many areas of life and spirituality. Even with physical healing prayer, many of us use one or more methods or protocols that we have developed as a result of learning what usually does and does not work. When we do certain things a certain way, we find that our level of efficacy in healing ministry increases. On the other hand, it is possible to rely too closely on a method such that we don't listen the Holy Spirit leading and guiding us as we pray. The best option is to be Spirit-led combined with use of a protocol, giving us a launching point but eventually proceeding forward in a subjective manner based on the situation. In the same way as we do with physical healing, we want to use methods or protocols of courtroom work as a launching pad into new experiences, not as rigid guidelines we must follow to the letter each time.

When entering into the Heavenly Courts via protocol, we have to watch out for highly legalistic methods that place us under new forms of religious bondage. This often looks like a set of teachings that start by getting us better results and seem like freedom, but over time they morph into a to-do list of "things we have to do" to keep measuring up. Sometimes the method itself is perfectly fine, but the group using it is the problem. I have met both individuals and groups who communicate in such a way that you start to feel as though you are somehow falling behind spiritually if you haven't kept up with the latest method or recently engaged in some sort of *court-work*. What may have started out as a process to bring greater liberty has then devolved into a group-think mindset complete with both verbal and nonverbal expectations to remain an active and accepted member of the group. While the initial method may still be extremely helpful, the overall religious atmosphere has become stifling, and what was once empowering is now bondage-creating.

In all honesty, this is not limited to the Courts Teaching and is something that happens in almost any system of thought or methodology designed for life-transformation. There are all sorts of diets, exercise programs, network marketing groups, and other organizations that ultimately start out on the right track but over time devolved into legalistic systems that are almost cultish in their need to police people into adhering to The System. My point here is that while this is not unique to this teaching, it is something you are likely to encounter as you go deeper and learn more about this concept. On the other hand, the fact that the enemy has led some people off-target by way of legalistic mindsets in no way negates the effectiveness of the actual methods themselves. Methods work, which is why some people turn them into new religious subsystems.

The Method

Let us now look at a basic method for engaging in Courtroom prayer to give an idea of how this can be done. When I go into the spirit to hold a court session, I begin by appearing in the courtroom itself. Because God is omniscient and already knows what I am doing (since the spirit realm is timeless to begin with), I operate under the expectation that I don't have to explain to anyone present why I am there—I simply presume the court proceedings will start, and they do.

The typical court process itself is generally very simple and can be broken down into four steps:

1. Accusation
2. Repentance
3. Forgiveness
4. Ruling (aka Victory)

Now let us review what this looks like in-process. If I am addressing an area of life where the enemy is coming against me, the court session usually starts with the enemy accusing me of wrongdoing. There are two ways this can be done. First, one can do his or her best to attempt to hear in the spirit what the enemy is saying against them. This can be easy for some, but more difficult for others, and the level of difficulty may also vary in each situation. If you are unable to hear in the spirit what the enemy is saying, don't worry about it and go with the second option. This method is where I don't bother to listen to the enemy to begin with—not because it is wrong, but because this part of the proceeding sometimes seems unnecessary to me, and also because I can be impatient, so I skip the step as I see fit. I call this the Ignore Method, because I don't really care what the enemy is saying since in a little while the blood of Jesus is going to nullify the accusation anyway. The whole point of hearing accusations from the enemy is to uncover contributing factors to how the enemy is gaining access into my life to afflict me. Because we have revelation from Holy Spirit, we can often get that information without listening to the enemy prattle on about it, so it all depends on how I feel led by the Spirit as to how I proceed. It is fair to note that results will vary using either method for this step.

The next step, repentance, can be done by the leading of Holy Spirit whether one heard a single accusation or not. In this phase, we renounce and verbally repent for anything we see we have done to welcome the enemy's actions in our lives. Some could argue that repentance is an action of turning in the right direction, not a verbalization, and that is true. However, an apology is a form of active repentance, moving from the wrong direction into the right one. Sometimes we cannot reverse a situation, but we can acknowledge our error or wrongdoing and attempt to make it right. The same applies here.

It can also be argued that we do not welcome the enemy's attention in our lives and that the demonic attack us because they are lawbreakers. While this is true to a certain extent, in that the enemy *are* lawbreakers, we still do create realms of access in our lives. We attract both positive and negative forces into our existence through our thoughts and actions. When we engage in sinful, dark, or evil thoughts, we literally send out a spiritual attractive force that demons are drawn to. Likewise, when we send out thoughts of light, life, and love, we attract the influence of the angelic realms. In other words, when demons gain influence, it is typically through partnership *with* us, not all on their own. This is why when casting a demon out of someone that demon might claim that it was invited in. While conveniently leaving out a very large portion of the story, it is not entirely wrong. Repentance negates, in part, the influence and access we have given the enemy by ending the alignments we have made with them through our choices. Sometimes this is referred to as *breaking agreements* or *closing doors*, but regardless of what someone calls it, we are putting a stopping point on the access we have helped create between ourselves and the demonic realms.

The third step, forgiveness, is where we call Jesus up to the stand to speak into the situation—which really just means He testifies on our behalf. We have to remember that Jesus is 100% on our side, and He intercedes constantly on our behalf before the throne of God (Hebrews 7:25). Jesus is like our yes-man when it comes to forgiveness of sin. In fact, it is impossible for Jesus *not* to forgive our sin because He already did it on the cross at Calvary a few thousand years ago. Furthermore, since He is the lamb who was slain from before the foundations of the world (Revelation 13:8), which means he was slain before the moment of conception of time and space, our sins have been dealt with in eternity. Therefore, having been forgiven in eternity, no accusations can stand strong against the blood of Jesus inside the time-realm. Usually I take this time during the court proceedings to ask Jesus if he has forgiven every aspect of my sin, poor decisions, and wrongdoing, and when he replies, "Yes," I have no further questions—what else is there to know? When Jesus' blood forgives something, it forgives it fully and completely—forever.

After Jesus takes the stand as *the* Expert Witness and exonerates me, I request the judge for a ruling. While this is the fourth and final Step in the court proceeding, it's almost entirely ceremonial because predictably, the judge *always* rules on my behalf. And that's a large part of what makes the Courts of Heaven so effective—the odds are ever in our favor! In reality the heavenly courts can't rule any other way, because to do so would be to ignore the finished work of Jesus on the cross—no one in all of heaven would be so foolish as to rule in opposition to the will of the King of Kings.

This is just one basic method and is useful for dealing with areas in our lives that leave openings to enemy attack. This four-step process can be applied to almost anything that isn't going right, and it can be done on behalf of someone else. When doing courtroom prayer for someone else, some people have an elaborate breakdown of who you can and cannot do it for based on some series of regulations, but I personally find it much more simple—either I can repent on behalf of others or I cannot. If I cannot, the process is irrelevant to try for others, and if it is possible, then anyone is fair game. When in doubt, keep things simple, and always be led by Holy Spirit. If you do that, you can't go wrong.

After giving you a basic method for engaging in Courts of Heaven prayer via spirit travel, I want to share with you a court session I went into back in August of 2015 to give one example of what this could look like. For those who might be unclear about the perspective I am coming from during this court case, I firmly believe that when Jesus said all throughout the book of John that we who believe in Him will live forever and not die, that He meant it literally, not as a heaven-when-you-die reality. This reality is alluded to all throughout the Scriptures, and I believe that this gospel of Jesus

Christ that we preach and believe in is a gospel of life and immortality, the same gospel the Apostle Paul believed, preached, and taught (2 Timothy 1:10-11).

During this court session, I traveled back into the Courts of Heaven where an angel had brought me one time prior. The goal of this session was to put myself in the custody of Holy Spirit, the Spirit of Life, and to disavow attachments I had made to the spirit of Death. The court session began with an unknown individual presiding over the case, but I was clear that this was a human, presumably from the cloud of witnesses, not the Father, an angel, or other heavenly being.

I took my seat at a table on the right side, facing the bench, and Death was located at a table to my left. There was no jury, as this was essentially a custody hearing and I was seeking to change custodians. I was invited by the judge to speak and explain why I was seeking this court hearing. I explained that I did not understand when I was younger that I did not have to die, and so I made many statements, held beliefs, and engaged in actions that aligned myself with Death and I had unknowingly placed myself in its care. I went on to state that as I now understand that I do not have to die that I wish to be released from Death's custody.

The spirit of Death then stood up and had the opportunity to speak. When I looked at it, I saw this thin spectre that had ill-defined, smoky black features. Its voice was ugly as it sounded its accusations to the judge with a hiss, stating that because I had chosen it that I was its rightful property. After it gave a short speech, it sat back down.

Next, I saw a man holding a scroll approach the judge's bench— it was Jesus. He unfurled this scroll before the judge and they had a short conversation which I could not hear. I couldn't read the scroll but I understood that it was basically a writ stating that I had been fully bought and covered by Jesus' blood, and that as a result, Death had no rightful hold over me. This was all the evidence that was needed, and after the judge saw that, he called me up to the witness stand to testify. This was my opportunity to declare and decree in the heavens what my intentions were for the future.

In the spirit I got up on the stand and I stated that I now believe that I am not destined to die, but to live forever. I acknowledged that while I once believed I had to die when I was younger, I have since learned the truth and have come to accept that reality. I stated that I no longer consider myself under custody to death and place myself in custody of the Spirit of Life. I collectively broke agreement with every belief, mindset, and understanding that I had previously held that said I would get sick or had to die. I renounced as a collective whole every statement I had made or that anyone else had made that has cursed me to be sick or die in any way, or that I have agreed with about the hold that death has over me and others. I stated that I am no longer allowed to die, but if for any reason I ever were to die, that I would resurrect immediately unless the Lord wanted to show me something in the heavens first, but if I were to ever die that I would always, *always* come back to life. After I finished my testimony, which was again more of a decree for the future rather than testifying as a witness on the stand, the judge banged the gavel once and declared that my custody had changed hands.

One more thing happened right before the case was dismissed. I could not clearly see the being who served as my counsel (though I believe it was Holy Spirit), but He petitioned the judge for a transfer of property from Death to me. My Counsel explained that because Death had stolen from me that I was entitled to a seven-fold return for what was taken. The judge instantly granted this petition without hearing further testimony from the opposition, assigned a bailiff of the court to go carry out this decree, then ended the case.

With the court case over, Death stalked out of the room, but he was actually hobbling now—as though some sort of force had been taken from him and he was now weaker. A man who glowed with golden light approached me and introduced himself as Isaac. He did not state such, but I understood by revelation that he was the Isaac in the Old Testament, Abraham's son. I had trouble looking at him, so he dimmed the light of glory emanating from him, and while I still could not see his features clearly, his hair appeared brown, his face was somewhat rounded in shape, and he was shorter than me. He explained that he had a few things to share with me. First, he told me that while I was not at that point yet, as I continued down this path of immortality that at a certain point, my cells themselves would literally undergo a transformation. I had a vision of what he was saying as he was speaking, and it showed me where my cells literally transformed from normal cells into vibrant, golden-glowing cells that emanated life-energy and had no speck of sickness or disease in them.

He then escorted me to a garden, which he said was my garden in heaven. It was spacious and beautiful, with much lush greenery that was landscaped quite beautifully, with a gazebo in the part of the garden that I saw. We turned, and Isaac showed me a young tree, approximately five to six feet tall, that had two or three pieces of oblong, pear-like fruit on its branches. "This is a tree of life. Take a bite of the fruit," he said. I picked one and took a bite. It was juicy, and as I ate it, I could feel a message being sent to my cells in my physical body to dump toxins and other garbage they had been holding. I could feel my intestines beginning to churn slightly. At his instruction I took two more big bites, then he told me to plant the core in the ground, which I did a short distance from the other one in an empty space. I understood that a new tree was going to grow from it, and that because life in heaven is so abundant that even the fruit wasn't going to decay but rather would remain intact underground yet still have the tree grow out of it. From there, Isaac took me to a mountain which he said was my mountain—my property. Stored inside were a great many things, but he took me to a room that was filled with scrolls and other writings.

The room was jam-packed, but everything was in disorder. Random scrolls and rolls of paper were piled on things and papers were spilling out of filing cabinets, as well as various piles on the table and other surfaces. He explained that there was a lot of revelation present in me, but that because everything was so cluttered that there was revelation I had received that I haven't even realized because it is hidden under the piles of disorganization. He instructed me to work on "cleaning up" so that everything would become more organized. I had a vision of a small, half-sheet-sized piece of glowing golden paper that was sitting on the floor somewhere, and that while I could see this paper in the vision, it was hidden under other things and that as I cleaned, I would find it. At the time, I took this part of the message to mean that I needed to clean up how I have my computer files organized of all the prophetic words, dreams, and other revelation that God has given me so that it is more accessible, but I believe there must be more. From there the experience ended.

This encounter began in the Courtroom but expanded outward after the fact into a garden and a mountain—*my* garden and mountain! That travel experience alone covers much more than I can explain here, but I hope this gives you not only a picture of what a case in the Courts of Heaven might look like, but a glimpse of some of the other things that are possible to encounter in the spirit realm.

Other Thoughts

My method and subsequent court case example is just one of the many ways this teaching can be applied. For example, mine was a spiritual custody hearing, whereas someone else might not have a custody issue but rather a real-life marriage problem, problematic personal behavior, property dispute, demon attack, or any other issue needing resolution. There are also what might be considered more advanced versions of this type of prayer including teachings on *which* courts people are allowed to go in, having to do with their specific petition, maturity level, level of authority in the spirit, or other extenuating circumstances. While these advanced versions don't necessarily rub me the wrong way, some of them do not quite sit right with me either. The reason is that as we delve deeper into the Courts of Heaven teachings, I have found that a sort of spiritual elitism can creep in.

I touched on this briefly earlier in the chapter, but this elitist approach often hides under the guise of a "You need to do it *this* way" attitude, promoting strict adherence to certain rules, regulations, and methodologies. The posture that comes with this approach is as if one wrong step is going to bring about judgment upon us in the spirit realm through the very heavenly court system that is supposed to bring us into greater freedom and which is theoretically stacked in our favor. Jesus did speak about prayer from a perspective of a heavenly legal system, but at the core of what He came to do was to set us free from the law of sin and death. Anything, no matter how life-giving it tends to be, can be perverted into a legalistic system that brings us into bondage with rules that are enticing because they seem so much more spiritually advanced than whatever we were doing previously. Not only that, but Holy Spirit will at times confirm to us what God is doing through these legalistic systems, even encouraging us to enter into them, long before we see the problems inherent within. This is not because God is giving his stamp of approval on the bondage-mindsets, but rather the system meet a need in our lives at that time, but that doesn't negate the need to sift out the religious and legalistic thinking as we learn and grow in any area, even if God leads us there. Keep in mind that not all teaching that goes deeper than I have shared here is elitist or restrictive. This is meant to be a reminder that there are some ditches out there to avoid, and as with all things spiritual, wisdom and discernment must be used as we learn and grow.

One other perspective to consider is that we should remember that we are heirs of God and coheirs with Christ, and we are being taught to rule and reign with Him, which means we don't always have to come into the courts as a supplicant seeking redress. Rather, we also have the right to legislate things as the one sitting *in* the judge's seat. Oftentimes when I am in the spirit, I operate from my authority and decree things to get accomplished in the earth, not beg God in a spiritual courtroom to do something He already legally established through Jesus Christ. At times, I almost have to work at it to put myself in a subservient position as the supplicant instead of finding myself sitting *as* the judge doing the legislating.

Where this subject of the Courts gets confusing is when we look at the fact that while yes, we will judge angels, it is entirely possible that if there are a vast number of different courtrooms in heaven, many of them may be run by spirit beings other than God—including angels, heavenly elders, and possibly even those in the cloud of witnesses who have gone on before us. While at first this might seem strange to some, a number of places in the *Bible* discuss the difference between mature and immature children of God and the resulting authority afforded each, which has bearing on this matter. Without going into too much detail here, I want to share a short excerpt from my book *Faith To Raise The Dead* that explains this concept.

> Galatians 4:1-2 explains it like this, "What I am saying is that as long as an heir is underage, he is no different from a slave although he owns the whole estate. The heir is subject

to guardians and trustees until the time set by his father." In other words as God's children, we have to have others watch over us—and not just other believers, but Holy Spirit and even the angels to help us grow into maturity. In the same way that we wouldn't let a three year old have full reign of the house, likewise God doesn't necessarily give us everything without some limitations early on. This isn't to keep us from things, but to safeguard us until we mature.

This idea holds true when studied out in the Scriptures. The New Testament uses a few different words that usually translate as "child"—the words nepios, teknon, and huios. A nepios son is basically an infant or young child and needs constant supervision. A teknon child is like those mentioned in Galatians 4:1-2 above—one who still needs an authority figure to watch over him and help him with daily affairs, but who is no longer a baby. A huios son (or daughter) has become a mature member of his household and is able to wield the full authority he possesses as an heir.

The Scriptures speak of sons and daughters of God operating in authority at differing levels based on our maturity. When we understand this, the idea that God might set heavenly judicial bodies in place to rule over us starts to make a bit more sense. At the very least I can see scriptural precedent that makes room, at least in the short term, for God to set angels or other spirit beings in charge from a judicial-ruling perspective.

I share this because I believe we can have a lot of pre-formed ideas in any direction based on the teachings we have been exposed to regarding exactly how a Court session is supposed to go, but when it comes time to put them in action, pretty much anything can happen. It is possible to encounter one's own soul fragments in court, or have an angel, ancestor, or other being that is not the Father presiding over the court proceedings. It is possible that we might find ourselves in different courtrooms depending on the situation, and God may give us wisdom and guidance on what that looks like for specific circumstances. On the other hand, Holy Spirit may never teach us a single thing about how to know which courtrooms to use because we always appear in the right place. Depending on who you talk to that could be a sign of immaturity and not properly learning how the system works, or a sign of maturity because you understand that spirit realm interaction is largely guided by the will. When you will yourself to appear in the right place, you usually end up where you seek to be whether you have been there before or not. If you wish to be in the *correct* court room, a mature son or daughter might simply appear at the right one always because his or her faith makes it occur in that manner.

There is a bit of a debate going on in circles where Courtroom Prayer is used as to whether people are limited in where we are permitted to go, whether only certain people are allowed or *called* to appear in certain courts, and also whether we can go to the wrong courtrooms or not—to the point that some individuals are literally telling others, "You aren't authorized to appear in this or that courtroom." As I was trying to tease out my own thoughts on this subject and figure out how to address it here, I did what I often do— phone a friend. Sometimes talking things out with others helps me reach greater clarity, so I gave a call to my friends Praying Medic and his wife—both of whom had really good wisdom to share in response to my growing concerns about some of the legalism that has entered this teaching. While not directly cited as an interview due to the conversational format of our discussion and my inability to separate which ideas came from whom, much of the material in the rest of this chapter is derived from our collective discussion as well as my further consideration of the subject after the fact. *Author's Note: None of the ideas below should be quoted as or understood to be the view of Praying Medic and/or his wife.*

The issue of whether people are allowed in certain courts or whether only those who are called to the Courts should attempt it or not is a confusing subject, partly because there are different views and everyone has a different answer. First off, the basic Courtroom prayer method that I have shared thus far is literally for everyone, and is simply a method to actively apply the redemptive power of Jesus Christ into our lives via spirit travel. If it wasn't, then salvation wouldn't be for everyone either. Every human on the planet is given free access to His redemptive work, so suggesting that someone is not supposed to be in that particular Court is absurd. On the other hand, God does take us through a process of growth and maturity, so it is possible that other courtrooms which deal with legislating various matters into the spiritual or natural realms, could be off-limits to some people based on where they are currently at in their growth process, although that could always change at a later date.

What I just said could sound exclusionary, but if we look at God's inclusive nature, and recall His desire to help us grow and mature as His sons and daughters, that we can reach an understanding of how this elitist-sounding court-process works that most closely aligns with His heart. First, we must consider that anything from God that is restrictive in nature is always *for* us, not to keep things from us. While there may be restrictions on who appears in some courts, it is a positive thing, not discriminatory, and access to those courts is something God will confirm to each of us individually, not something that another human has the right to tell us whether we are allowed to or not.

In reality, those aren't simply courtrooms either, but a function of a spiritual legislative body. In the same way that we have elected and appointed officials in human governments, the heavens operate similarly. Not everyone is welcome simply because not every possesses the necessary qualifications for that specific matter and not all Courts in that regard are made equal. Sometimes it comes down to interest and other times to calling. I also think that we have many choices as to what we are *called* to, and a significant part of calling has to do with our response. In other words, if I have a potential calling to twenty different things but focus on two, the other eighteen will take a back seat until such time as I get around to them. Furthermore, there may be one thing I simply never get to, and at that point God will simply pass it on to someone else who has the interest in that area and who will follow through.

I personally believe the Courts of Heaven are real and important, but even if I have the calling for it, I lack both the time and present interest for deeper pursuit. This is largely because I am currently pursuing a calling in other areas, leaving me with less energy and ability to divide my attention to pursue the depths of the Courts. My own lack of focus and pursuit, therefore, dictates how deep I go at this time, but as the future holds new things for us all, I believe I may engage the legislative aspect of the Courts at a later time. In the end, everyone has access to the basic-level of the Court system, but the legislative aspects may or may not be for everyone.

There is another related issue that sometimes keeps people from even attempting Court-work to begin with—the idea that we have to know a bunch of things before we start doing anything, because if we don't know enough, we could mess things up. This particular teaching is both erroneous and harmful to the Body of Christ. In Matthew 23:13 Jesus said, "Woe to you, teachers of the law and Pharisees, you hypocrites! You shut the door of the kingdom of heaven in people's faces. You yourselves do not enter, nor will you let those enter who are trying to." This faulty teaching does the same thing Jesus berated the Pharisees for—it *shuts the door of the kingdom of heaven* by making people afraid to ascend into the heavens without having a long list of items lined up first. This is the opposite of God's goal, and as such, this teaching is anti-Christ in nature.

The fact is we all mess up when we try new things. It is unavoidable and the Courts are no different. When we first set foot in the Courts of Heaven, we know little of what we are doing, and God gives us much grace. He doesn't expect us to learn a bunch of things before we engage the heavenly realms, and God isn't restricting our access until we "have it all figured out," so don't let that keep you from trying. As we learn new things, including protocol on how to proceed, we simply use that information the next time we go without condemnation for not knowing it prior. This is all part of the learning process and God factors our growth into our heavenly interactions.

Along with this issue of "doing things right," is the concern over whether or not we can end up in the wrong courtroom. Some people believe that if we aren't careful to do things correctly that we can end up in the wrong courtroom in the spirit realm and then somehow bring judgment upon ourselves as a result. I have a few thoughts on this.

The idea that if we do things wrong then we will end up in the wrong place and make problems worse is both fear-inducing and poorly founded. We have to remember that we travel to the Heavenly Courts by matter of will. If you think you are in the wrong place, just mentally choose to end up in the right place and you'll be fine. If you don't know what the "right place" is, simply desiring to be in "the right place" will suffice—you should end up there. You can't really mess it up—the courtroom is completely stacked in your favor and Jesus' blood is the argument that wipes out all opposition. I did hear of a circumstance where someone ended up in the "wrong court" once, but it was because instead of seeking justice in a situation and to remove the influence of the enemy, he was seeking to place judgment on someone else. The case got moved from one court to another, but the move was to a demonic courtroom presided over by a pagan god. In other words, he wanted to go to a heavenly courtroom, but in name only. He went with wrong motives, seeking to level judgment against another party, which is the work of the enemy, not our Father in heaven. Whether he realized it or not, he was actually seeking to engage the enemy, and succeeded in doing so. Even in this situation God gave him grace such that he got out of that courtroom once he realized what was going on. The point I am making here is that where we go in the spirit at any given moment is mainly dictated by a combination of our intention of where to go, our motives as we do so, and our inner beliefs as a whole. There are other factors, but these three are the main ones. This man's intention took him to a court, but his motives took him to a demonic one.

I suggest that sort of thing is extremely uncommon. Generally, if we want to end up in a specific courtroom, we are going to arrive there. If by some strange reason we ended up in the wrong place in the heavens, I assume someone in the heavens should be intelligent enough to point us in the right direction. I have to imagine that the judge presiding over that courtroom is going to direct us properly instead of a much more illogical option—going ahead with a court case they don't have jurisdiction over to begin with because it's the wrong court. Even an incompetent judge wouldn't do that on the earth, so why do we think it would happen in the heavens? Honestly, we need to demystify things a little and take some of the fear out of Heavenly Courtroom proceedings because it not only is unwarranted, it confuses people and makes things needlessly difficult.

When someone feels he or she has ended up in the wrong courtroom, what is more likely is he ended up in a *false courtroom*. One of the things I and many others have discovered doing inner healing work is the existence of false Jesuses. These are spirits that pretend to be Jesus but in reality are demons leading us astray. When we encounter them during inner healing prayer, it makes it harder to accurately discern what God is doing—because the very Person we think we can trust, Jesus, turns out to be an imposter. Likewise, if someone encounters a courtroom in the spirit that places him under deeper bondage, it probably was not a Heavenly one but pretended it was. The Heavenly courts do *not* put people under bondage no matter what horror stories one may have heard. This is one of the reasons why discernment is so key when engaging the spiritual realms—things are not always as they appear. One might then want to know how we can objectively know when it is a real courtroom or a false one, and there is no concrete, impartial way to know. We have to try and learn, mess up on occasion, and grow our discernment from both our positive and negative experiences—that's how it is for everyone; there are no shortcuts to cultivating discernment.

At the end of the day, there are probably as many different methods as there are people using them, so it is important to not get so tied into a single way of doing things that we lose the ability to be flexible and change with things as they evolve. At one point God might make things incredibly simple, to turn around later and make them more complex, and when we have delved deep into the complexities of things, He may flip it all on its head and simplify our methods yet again. Jesus said in John 10:29, "My Father, who has given them to me, is greater than all; no one can snatch them out of my Father's hand." What is certain, regardless of what and how we proceed, is that God's ability to keep us is greater than the enemy's ability to lead us astray. If we remain open to being led and guided by Holy Spirit at all times, then we really can't go wrong.

Chapter 12

The Ethics of Spirit Travel

A saying that is best known for being attributed to Uncle Ben from *Spiderman* is, "With great power comes great responsibility." Luke 12:48b says essentially the same thing but with different language: "From everyone who has been given much, much will be demanded; and from the one who has been entrusted with much, much more will be asked." It is not enough to be able to travel in the spirit. We have a responsibility to use this ability wisely, and to do so in an upright and ethical manner.

Back in 2007, I had a friend, Georgia, who was having problems with an unwanted suitor. This unwanted suitor styled himself a prophet. He was new to the church and began to make relational claims on her in his comments to her circle of friends—as if to let them all know that she was his property. As I discovered at that time, some prophets and other spiritually advanced people knew how to do a *lot* more in the spirit realm than they taught publically. In fact, I would be very surprised if the vast *majority* of prophets and prophetic people haven't displayed only a portion of their spiritual abilities out of fear of rejection from the Church. While on the one hand I think it is somewhat unethical to go around speaking about spiritual realities everywhere but hiding the "deeper" truths, I do believe a shift is taking place and more people are getting braver, sharing more of the revelation God has given them and disregarding popular opinion. This shift has allowed the Body of Christ to begin discussing and teaching on spirit travel openly—something that certainly did not happen ten to fifteen years ago.

At any rate, this guy who was after my friend was one of the ones who knew how to engage the spiritual realms—to the point where he had taken to spying on her in the spirit. She discerned what he was up to and didn't like it, and called the only people she trusted that she also thought would be able to help her: my wife and me. The Holy Spirit had only given me a taste of this ability to perceive details about other people from afar, a sort of far-sight or spiritual spying, a week or two prior. I did not have much experience to draw on, but I did know that this ability, as with most everything in the spirit, is largely directed by our will. Armed with what little I had, my wife and I joined Georgia in prayer to fend off these unwanted spiritual intrusions.

This process of prayer over her went on for at least a week or two, and during this period there was one occasion where my wife and I both felt uneasy about Georgia's safety. We began to intercede for her, but also did something practical—we called her. She wasn't answering her cell phone, and not knowing what else to do, I finally went in the spirit to check in on her. I was not incredibly comfortable doing so at the time as I knew that we were basically doing the same thing her unwanted suitor was doing, but having perceived a very real danger to her well-being, not having her home address, and with no other options, I did so anyway. She was fine, and I was glad God had shown me how to do this so I was able to check on her in that way. We did tell her after the fact what we had done and why, and she was fine with it, considering it was out of love in order to protect her.

There was a key difference between what I did and what this "prophet" was doing. In his case, he was using this ability for selfish and even wicked purposes, whereas when I did so, it was with pure motives and without secrecy. This scenario is just one example of the kinds of things that can happen if we do not pay attention to how we use the abilities at our disposal through traveling in the spirit. I have spoken with other friends who have shared similar stories of people who have decided to use their spiritual gifts inappropriately.

When discussing spiritual ethics, it can be difficult to know exactly what to do and not to do, because what might be permissible for one person would be completely unacceptable for another. Furthermore, if we try to lay out a hard set of rules then we are no different than the Law of rules and regulations Jesus died to set us free from. God doesn't want us bound by rules, and no amount of regulatory statutes will actually fix bad behavior. It is far better for us to learn the principles behind how to spirit travel in an ethical manner, practicing how to be both polite and respectful of others.

In the simplest of terms it comes down to emulating the fruit of the spirit—love, joy, peace, patience, kindness, goodness, faithfulness, gentleness, and self-control (Galatians 5:22-23). I would say this list could go a bit further though, pulling in a list that Paul wrote in Philippians 4:8-9, which says:

> Finally, brothers and sisters, whatever is true, whatever is noble, whatever is right, whatever is pure, whatever is lovely, whatever is admirable—if anything is excellent or praiseworthy—think about such things. Whatever you have learned or received or heard from me, or seen in me—put it into practice. And the God of peace will be with you.

If we want to engage spiritual abilities in an upright manner, then we will focus on doing only those activities that are noble, admirable, lovely, and so on. If we do things in such a manner we can trust that as we sow this behavior out that we will reap in like kind—the God of peace will be with us, and He will bring peace into our spiritual interactions. In the same way that Georgia was unhappy about her suitor's unwanted attention and yet perfectly fine with my well-meaning snooping that was done out of love, we will most often receive this same grace from others if our motives are pure and our methods praiseworthy.

It is easy to think of what not to do—anything that involves invading the privacy of others, attempting to harm them in some way, or in any way treating them other than you believe they would want to be treated. Spying on people for perverted means is obviously problematic. I had a single encounter when the Lord was teaching me about how to use this ability where I was downstairs in my wife's house and could see another married couple (who lived there) upstairs in the shower together. I didn't initiate it to begin with, and the biggest problem was that at first *I couldn't get it to stop.* What I now realize is that the demonic were activating this ability that was so new to me, and I believe were trying to get me to swear it off out of fear of illicit use. My wife and I prayed and I was able to end the visionary experience after a minute or so, but I had to spiritually fight to be able to do so. Since this gift operates by our will, it is generally under our control. After all, 1 Corinthians 14:32 says, "The spirits of prophets are subject to the control of prophets." Thus, we must exercise self-control when using it. Any time we find ourselves having difficulty starting or stopping spirit travel, visions, or similar spiritual experiences, it reveals demonic interference at work, and we must pray to break the power of the enemy. If this happens to someone regularly, inner healing and deliverance are recommended since most likely the enemy has some measure of access in a person's life to be able to pervert this God-given gift. One other possibility is that we have a fragment or alter (a fragment that has more consciousness and/or self-awareness) who serves the demonic. I know people who were unaware they had alters who were witches and actively cast spells in the spiritual dimensions on the core self and other fragmented parts. Because an alter that serves the enemy is actually part of one's soul, that alter has special access to make agreements with the enemy that our core self might never agree to.

I would like to share some good guidelines (not rules) to operate by if we are unsure of how to use our ability to travel in the spirit. First, we are free to travel into the heavenly realms. The *Bible* says that we are already seated there (Ephesians 1:3, Ephesians 2:6-7), and God does not place limitations on us in that regard. In fact, Hebrews 4:16 tells us to come *boldly* before the throne of grace to find help when we have needs. If God is telling us to come boldly before His throne, He is not limiting our ability to travel into the heavenly realms where His throne is located. Some places might not be particularly safe, depending on what part of the spirit realms you are traveling through, so use wisdom as you do so—just know that you have open access.

Sometimes when we surrender ourselves to the Lord in times of prayer, He will take us where He wants us to go. In situations such as this, it isn't an issue of whether we have permission or not—Holy Spirit is leading the parade and we are simply following Him and doing what we see Him doing. When I was in that ministry school in 2007, it was during a time of intercession for an end-of-year mission trip to India that I found myself unexpectedly taken in the spirit in an in-body experience somewhere in that nation. I presumed I was brought somewhere we were going to go, but I had no way of knowing that in advance. The best I could tell, it was a stall or shop in a marketplace, with an open-air storefront. Inside the stall was dark and I was unable to see further, and then the experience faded out. Things changed for me shortly after that and I never ended up going on the mission trip, so I have no idea if I would have visited that shop or not, but the fact remains that the Lord brought me into that encounter without any purposeful attempt on my part to engage spiritual travel, outside of a willingness to go.

Spirit travel as a whole is fine if we are doing anything in the heavens, in outer space, or even round and about in public places on the earth. It only becomes a real ethical issue if we are spying on people, in some way crossing personal boundaries, or directly disobeying God's specific directions to us in that moment. It is fine to do whatever the Lord is leading us to do. If God is leading me to go in the spirit and do something, such as lay hands on someone who is sick, then I already have His permission to do it and thus crossing someone's boundaries isn't an issue at that time.

Permission really is pretty important from an ethical standpoint. It is a little like having a stranger walk into your house without ringing the doorbell or knocking. If a friend does it, you might still feel intruded upon but because you have a relationship with them, you may be willing to overlook the offense or easily address it with them. Yet again, other friends might be so close to you that you have already told them where you hide your secret key and have instructed them to just let themselves in whenever they like. It all depends on the relationship you have with the person in question. This should be considered carefully when traveling to and fro in the earth.

I once asked a group of friends for their thoughts on the subject of ethical spirit travel. While the responses were varied, most held a common thread, and we had a general consensus that we prefer to do it with other people only when we have their permission. Once, my friend Matt and I were practicing with one another over the phone, each attempting to travel to the other's location and describe the room each was in, but the key is that we did so willingly with one another. On rare occasion I will have a burden for someone who I haven't gotten permission from, so in those cases, I tend to consult with the Lord on the matter and get His go-ahead. I don't want to go where I am not welcomed.

If we are unsure, it is always best to ask God, but when we really are not sure how the Lord is leading us, we can typically trust and fall back on our motives to decide whether something is appropriate or not. One instance where I might do so without someone's express permission in advance is if I am interceding for them for healing. The key is that what I am doing is geared toward something they already need and want—healing. Additionally, I am not being overly intrusive or causing problems since I don't hang out in the spirit after the fact. Having said that, if I try to heal someone from a distance without asking, he or she has usually already requested prayer to begin with, which is why I am even interceding to begin with—I don't do it with everyone all the time.

For example, back when I was a CNA and I worked at this one hospital, one night the staff were watching a patient's breathing on a monitor; he was breathing *very* slowly. One of the nurses mentioned that she was uncomfortable with how slowly he was breathing, and that she thought someone should go poke him to rouse him a little more and cause him to breathe more rapidly. Not telling them, I simply went in the spirit into his room and smacked him, and within one *literal* second of doing that, I watched his breathing rate increase on the monitor in front of me. My motivation was not to harm him but to cause him to breathe better. Thus, I wasn't invoking some ungodly spirit or some such thing, but was saving myself the time and energy to walk across the entire unit to enter his room and rouse him, and was helping his breathing at the same time.

Another occasion while in that ministry school, I was at a worship party at someone's house. Well, more specifically it was a *get drunk in the Holy Spirit* party, and the hosts referred to it as the *Tasting Rooms*. A number of people were sitting in the living room, along with a handful of my ministry school peers, and on a whim I suggested we play a game of "hide-and-seek." I sent my spirit elsewhere in the house, and they had to go find me. Each of the other two students who were playing verbalized what they perceived my location to be to the group—they were both correct each time. A number of the other people present verbalized surprise and/or were impressed at our supposed elevated spiritual level, but it was really us just playing around in the spirit and doing something that anyone could do. In this instance it was fun, everyone who played had agreed to join in, and thus there were no moral or ethical issues that were involved.

Some people prefer to travel in the spirit only at the Lord's leading so as to keep themselves out of trouble and to ensure they remain upright in its use. I personally feel this is a limitation that would hold me back in experiencing all that God has for me, but there is nothing inherently wrong with this approach. A decision in this regard is governed largely by one's comfort level. Romans 14:23b says, ". . . everything that does not come from faith is sin." If you feel uncomfortable initiating spirit travel on your own, that is fine—continue to be led and guided by the Spirit as you are presumably doing now. If God wants to advance you beyond that someday, then He will let you know in His timing. Those of us who choose to do it on our own usually seek to be led by the Holy Spirit in our spiritual interactions as well; we simply don't always wait for God to initiate the encounter.

In engaging this spiritual ability, it is possible to search inside people, pry into their spirits and souls, and much more. As a general whole, it is always fine to be led in releasing what God is doing for someone in regards to inner healing and the like, but as one friend put it, sorting through their "dirty laundry" is something we should avoid unless we have permission. At the end of the day, use wisdom, seek guidance from Holy Spirit, and if there is any question as to whether something is appropriate or not, it is probably best to err on the side of caution and/or propriety and choose not to proceed. Ultimately it comes down to love and respect, and if we love and respect other people enough, we will not want to violate their privacy or trust, nor do anything we know they would not want. If there is only a single take-away from this chapter, let it be that we are to be led and guided by love in our spiritual interactions with one another.

Chapter 13

Trances

The *Bible* mentions multiple places where people had encounters with God and did so upon falling into a trance. While the term *trance* is not literally found in the *Bible*, the term is probably the most appropriate English approximation for what it does say, which we will review shortly. Trances are not often discussed in Christian circles, much less circles that practice spirit travel, but trances are actually quite common during in-body and out-of-body travel. As such, it is important to understand what they are, what they do, and how to recognize when they are happening.

Trances make an appearance in only one book of the *Bible*, the book of Acts. While this does depend a bit on the translator, the word *ekstasis*, which in Acts is translated as *trance*, appears only seven times in the New Testament, and is translated as either trance, amazement, or astonishment. It connotes the mind being in some sort of altered state due to a present experience. Thayer's Greek-English Lexicon defines *ekstasis* as:

> . . . a throwing of the mind out of its normal state,
> alienation of mind, whether such as makes a lunatic or that
> of a man who by some sudden emotion is transported as it
> were out of himself, so that in this rapt condition, although
> he is awake, his mind is drawn off from all surrounding
> objects and wholly fixed on things divine that he sees nothing
> but the forms and images lying within, and thinks that he
> perceives with his bodily eyes and ears realities shown him by
> God (Thayer).

This definition clearly shows that trances are altered states of consciousness such that instead of being focused on the material world, the mind has an otherworldly focus. From that definition it could give the impression that trances are always some sort of rapturous mind-altering experience, and in some cases they can be, but usually they are not. A trance can be something akin to that half-asleep half-awake state we all get in when tired and find ourselves saying nonsensical sentences that in our altered state seem perfectly normal until we wake up fully. It can be reached through meditation although this type of trance is normally considered a *light trance*— where the individual has the ability to open his or her eyes at any time and re-engage the physical world. In such instances there is usually a feeling of deep calm or peace within the body and mind while in and upon exiting the altered state.

Both Peter and Paul had trances which are recorded in Scripture. With Peter, it happened just before he was approached by some Gentiles whom God wanted to have hear the gospel. Acts 10:9-12 says:

> About noon the following day as they were on their
> journey and approaching the city, Peter went up on the roof

to pray. He became hungry and wanted something to eat, and while the meal was being prepared, he fell into a trance. He saw heaven opened and something like a large sheet being let down to earth by its four corners. It contained all kinds of four-footed animals, as well as reptiles and birds.

This trance was much like having a visionary encounter of some kind. In fact, Cornelius, just six verses prior, had a vision in which he spoke with an angel. While it did not explicitly state he was in a trance at the time, the encounter he had could easily have occurred that way.

With Paul, his trance occurred shortly after his conversion from persecuting the Christian Jews to becoming one of them. In Acts 22:17-18 Paul explained himself and this encounter, saying, "When I returned to Jerusalem and was praying at the temple, I fell into a trance and saw the Lord speaking to me. 'Quick!' He said. 'Leave Jerusalem immediately, because the people here will not accept your testimony about me.'" This trance Paul had also included spiritual instruction from the Lord. There are many other stories of people in the *Bible* who seem likely to have fallen into trances, including Saul among the company of prophets, Daniel when visited by the angel, Ezekiel when taken by the Spirit, Stephen when he was being stoned, the slave-girl with the spirit of divination who followed Paul, and the Apostle John when on Patmos, to name a few. These are, in theory, a much more common experience in the life of the believer than we have been taught, and are not something we should be afraid of.

Trances and trance states in and of themselves are simply states of consciousness and are neither godly nor demonic. In the same way that being asleep and awake are not specifically good or bad, neither are trances. Much the same as how a car, a gun, or almost anything can be used for good or ill, that has everything to do with the user, not the tool itself. In fact, it is quite common when casting demons out of people for the demon to put the person in a trance of some kind to try to keep from being cast out. Once a friend and I were sitting in my car praying, and as I began to pray for her, she slumped forward in the seat. I woke her up and prayed again, but she did the same thing. I recognized this as an attempt from the demonic, and addressed them until she stopped passing out. This sort of trance is unhelpful and has no inherent benefit.

On the other hand, I once worked with a woman who had trained enough to put herself in a light trance, which allowed us to do some needed inner healing work. As a nurse, she was one of my patients at the time. We had gotten to talking, and somehow we moved onto the subject of inner healing and multiple personalities. I had never worked with fragments and alters before, and this was the *night prior* to having my own first session with a prayer counselor to work with the same. Nevertheless, I decided to give it a shot and see where it led. The woman put herself into a light trance which allowed inexperienced me to get parts to come to the surface of her consciousness easily. We were able to make some good headway at that time. After some inner healing sessions with my own prayer counselor, I found that my own previously-developed ability to put myself in a light trance came in handy as it made it very easy to help the session move along, much as it had with that woman. While not necessarily the case for every prayer minister or ministry, I have found that skill helpful with this particular type of inner healing work.

Entering a trance state can be done in a few main ways, and anyone can train oneself to do it. One way is through meditation, typically Eastern meditation, and one can either recite some type of prayer or mantra over and over creating a sort of white-noise in the brain, or simply focus one's breathing and calm the mind. After doing this for a short while, the mind will become much more relaxed and at ease, and the body may even begin to feel like it is either floating or very heavy. These are potential signs one has entered into a light trance. On the other hand, I have found that when in such a state and the sensation is either mildly disorienting or there is a feeling of spacelessness or cloudiness or similar, this is often a demonic spirit trying to interfere in some way.

External devices can also be used to help enter a trance-state. Something called a *Binaural Beat* is a type of music or sound that can help alter the brainwaves to enter a trance-state. To understand this, we need to look at how the brain functions. According to the 11th Edition of *Principles of Anatomy and Physiology*, the neurons in the brain produce millions of electrical impulses at a time, and all together they are referred to as brain waves. These waves can be measured through a test called the electroencephalogram, or EEG. The brain has four types of waves, called the Alpha, Beta, Theta, and Delta respectively. Each wave oscillates at a certain frequency, known also as cycles per second, measured in hertz (Hz). Alpha waves run from 8-13 Hz and are common when awake but at rest. Beta waves run from 14-30 Hz and denote normal waking activity. Theta go from 4-7Hz and may be present during times of stress and/or brain disorders, while Delta range from 1-5 Hz and occur during deep sleep for adults or during normal wakefulness with infants (Tortora 500).

Binaural beats work by using sound to help target a certain hertz measurement of brainwaves. Because the low Hz levels needed to reach these states are inaudible, binaural beats use a method to trick the mind in entraining to those levels anyway by oscillating back and forth between two sound frequencies that are the exact number of Hz apart that the listener desires to reach. They have to be listened to with headphones because one frequency sounds in each ear and the alternation is what tricks the brain. For example, if one wanted to reach a theta state, say at 7 Hz, he might listen to a sound tuned to Major C, but two slightly different versions: one at437Hz and the other at 444Hz. They will be almost the exact same sound and many people would be unable to hear the difference, but the brain can tell. The sound itself, as one can imagine, is basically a droning noise, a bit like hearing a bee buzzing around, and often lower tones are used because they are less piercing to the ear and thus more comfortable to listen to.

This tool, and others like it, are just like trances—neither positive nor negative, all depending on how they are put to use. Healing sounds and frequencies are making a comeback due to their influence in healing the body, and certain sounds can help relieve emotional trauma as well. We already know that music can be soothing, aggravating, or even depressing, having a direct impact on the emotions of the listener. It is reasonable to assume that the altered state of the brain is in some way related to this response. For reasons unknown to this author, theta waves are attributed to assisting with astral projection, and those who practice it may make use of binaural beats to help put their brains into a state that is conducive to such travel. Whether one chooses to use binaural beats or not is entirely up to the reader, but there is nothing inherently spiritual about it one way or the other—it is listening to very boring music to help get into an appropriate mental state. It is not *owned* by any particular group, belief system, or ideology. Keep in mind this can be used to reach *any* of the four states, so sometimes people use it as a sleep aid. Rarely does one need help reaching the normal beta state (it's called *waking up*), so that is typically not found as a binaural beat.

Now that we have looked at what trances are and what they do, as well as how we can enter into them, how is this useful regarding spirit travel? I have found in my own life that going into a light trance helps me focus, which is especially helpful when practicing spirit travel. My mind is clear and extraneous thoughts do not interfere as readily, allowing me to pay full uninterrupted attention to the encounter before me. One of the easiest ways to enter into a light trance is to focus on one's breathing, taking slow deep breaths. Each time thoughts come up about other aspects of life, refocusing back on the sound, feel, and rate of breathing helps push those thoughts away. This is not so much *emptying the mind* as some like to call it, but I think of it as clearing out the clutter. I find that at times my mind is racing and my thoughts are all over the place; this approach helps me focus on what I want to be paying attention to without distractions. Breathing and pushing other thoughts away doesn't make one brainless, but it does allow us to enter into an encounter without disruption.

In the following chapter we will look at activation exercises designed to help us practice spirit travel. If practicing the above breathing exercise seems helpful, consider using it before starting the exercises to put yourself in an optimal state of mind for success.

Chapter 14

Activation Exercises

The goal of this chapter is to provide activation exercises to help you hone and advance your skills. Some of these are directly related to spirit travel while others are about honing the ability to see in the spirit. Any of these exercises can be beneficial, and all are shared in a step-wise format from foundational to advanced, but the reader is welcome to move around through them, skipping or altering parts as deemed necessary.

Before going into the exercises, it is important to gain some foundational understanding of how spirit travel actually functions—the nuts and bolts of the "how-to." The simple fact remains that God, when He set up the functional laws of the universe, made it so spiritual action is governed by will, and then He gave us free will, expecting that we would grow and mature to use it wisely. This opens up a potential can of worms about whether we are being led by God's will or directing things by our own will. Certainly we want our will to line up with His, but that's not a limiting factor regarding this subject. Our goal is always to be aligned with Him in everything we do; traveling in the spirit is certainly no different. If we just choose to always be aligned with Him, we can bypass further His-will-our-will discussion to look at the details of how our will influences the spirit realm.

When we talk about extending our will or using our will, the concept can seem a bit foreign because we tend to think of it as an abstract concept, not a concrete object or force. Other ways we can describe this are *intention*, *desire*, and *expectation*; all of these are closely related to our wishes, beliefs, thoughts, and faith. In fact, while our thoughts and desires are not quite the same thing, they both influence how, where, and why we travel in the spirit, as they are factors that influence our choices. Think of the will as a vehicle that is made up of various parts, and those parts are listed above. As we engage this vehicle and direct it toward a result, we receive that outcome. An example of this is when in the heavenly realms in the spirit and we decide to go to another location. We can either appear there instantly, or we can choose to go the long way and travel over land from point A to point B. Either is fine, but when we translocate instantly, it is because we have directed our will to cause us to appear there. In fact, much of spiritual reality functions on this same principle, and this carries over into spiritual warfare, inner healing and deliverance, and more.

If we want to engage spiritual reality we have to first believe we can, and then we have to choose to do so. With these two as a foundation, we can begin to visualize and imagine ourselves engaging the spiritual realms, which from there opens up into spiritual experiences. I will make one small point here. When we speak of going in the spirit, especially in the heavens, sometimes this is a visualization in our mind that is not necessarily altering spiritual reality, whereas other times we are truly engaging in the spirit realms. While there is no clear indicator to differentiate the two, I suggest that as we visualize and imagine, it naturally tips over into engaging spirit, so we don't need to stress much about whether it was "real" or "fake." If we engage the encounter then it is a real experience, and as we learn and grow in this area, we will learn to better differentiate between the two. Keep in mind that even in our own imaginings with God, we can have powerful encounters, receive deep inner healing, and more. At the end of the day none of it is really "fake," regardless of how the experience comes.

As we open ourselves up to the heavenly realms, we will gradually become more and more accustomed to doing this such that it becomes second nature, and easy. This is not, however, the starting point for most, so this chapter is intended to guide the reader forward.

"Target" Practice

I have included four sets of an exercise where you can practice what is sometimes termed as "remote viewing," another term related to the whole concept of spirit travel. As stated in a previous chapter, Remote Viewing officially began in the 1970s as part of the Stargate Project, a U.S. Government initiative to try to spy on other countries using psychic abilities and techniques. While the term Remote Viewing, or RV, has gained popularity in some circles, it is essentially a non-interactive form of spirit travel, and as such, there are techniques related to RV training one might find helpful while practicing spirit travel. While I have never been formally trained in remote viewing, I have learned a little about the subject, and many of the things I have learned as the Lord has taken me on this journey to traveling in the spirit have similarities.

The goal of this exercise is to practice directing the will toward perception of a person, place, idea, or object in order to gain information about it, honing the ability to accurately perceive. While

RV does not involve interacting with what we perceive, spirit travel does, and if we can perceive something correctly, we can more readily interact with it.

Number a sheet of paper one through ten. We are going to try to get information about ten people, places or objects that are unknown to us, and once we feel we receive information, to write it down. The lists to check answers are found in the appendix on page 189. Get comfortable, close your eyes if that helps, and clear your focus from other things. Take your time. There is no need to hurry with this exercise, and doing it quickly is not as important as doing it well. Next, going in order of one through ten, extend your expectation and desire outward, wanting to know what each number represents. Another way of describing this action is that you are extending your will to know. What this does is activate your inner ability to gather information spiritually. Go a step further and extend your expectation to actually *be* with the person, place, or thing you are trying to uncover.

The goal is to receive revelation about something entirely unknown, so as you receive revelation about each number, you will document your findings. As you expect revelation, think about the idea of number one and see if you have any visions. As you do this, note your observations. What colors and shapes do you see? What feelings or impressions do you get about the mystery number? Does a particular subject come to mind? Write all of these down, and when you feel you have enough, move to number two.

For example, let us pretend that target number one is Starry Night, the painting by Van Gogh. As you pray, you might see swirls in your vision, the colors blue or yellow, or even have a vision of stars in the sky. Since it is a painting, you might see a paint palette, a piece of wood representing the picture frame, or even a person in the act of painting. It is also possible you might see an art museum, or better yet, the Museum of Modern Art in New York where the painting resides. You might see the whole Starry Night painting—any of the above are possible, and all would be accurate in some manner, although some would obviously be more detailed than others.

Once you go through all ten numbers, check your answers to see how your perception matched up with the designated items, people, and locations. If you find your answers have some accuracy to them, nice work! If the revelation seems to be inadequate or lacking, consider what you can do differently next time. Are you focused or distracted? Look for ways to help promote clarity of mind. Could you be too tired? I have a harder time doing things like this when I am exhausted, and right before bed is either a great time for me to clear the thoughts of the day and focus, or it means I fall fast asleep and never get anywhere. Be mindful of what works for you. Does it feel like something is hindering your perception? If so, this may be an opportunity for inner healing and deliverance to free you to engage spiritual reality more readily in the future. Whatever the result, look at how you did well and consider what and how you can improve the next time.

The four lists in the Appendix I are the targets you will be using for practice. The first set you do should correspond with the first set of answers. The remaining three sets of targets will give you additional opportunities to practice these abilities. If you run out and want more, consider making up a set of flashcards from the items listed there, or create your own. Shuffle and mix them up, lay them out face down in front of you, and now you have all new lists! If you have a friend who can make targets for you, that is good too. Per the discussion on spirit travel ethics and etiquette in Chapter 12, I recommend picking nonliving subjects, and you will note that all of the people I chose are already deceased.

Correcting Your Vision

The next exercise is designed to help get you used to traveling outside of the body in a familiar location. First, close your eyes and visualize stepping outside of your body, walking to the far end of the room, and turning back to look at yourself and the room around you. Take a minute to do this, then open your eyes and look at what the actual room looks like. Do this exercise again, this time mentally correcting those things you saw the first time that do not accurately match the appearance of you and your surroundings.

Two Inner Healing Exercises

The next two exercises I have created first appeared on my blog in the article "DID Self-Healing: Integrating Fragments and Alters" and next as an upgraded version in a collaboration book on trauma titled *Broken to Whole: Inner Healing For the Fragmented Soul.*

These methods are designed to bring inner healing to fragments and alters as discussed briefly in Chapter 7, but it also works well to help familiarize one with both the inner spiritual world and spirit travel as a whole. While I have not discussed the inner spiritual world in any length in this book, consider that we all have realms of the spirit inside us, even as Luke 17:21b says, ". . . behold, the kingdom of God is within you" (KJV). The first part of this exercise brings the reader into the inner world where fractured parts reside to help heal them, and the latter version is designed to bring one into the heavenly realms to do the same, setting those captive parts free. Try either or both as you feel most applicable. Be aware that because these are inner-healing methods, it is possible to experience both inner healing and increased emotional turmoil as things are brought to the surface during the healing process. If you feel stuck or overwhelmed at this point, my book *Broken to Whole: Inner Healing For the Fragmented Soul* will provide you the tools needed and provide a launching pad for greater freedom.

The Fragment Plane

Begin by imagining a large space with a platform in the center. On that platform is a pillar of gold or blue light, with a small version of yourself in the middle. This is your "core self." Next, envision the many unintegrated or unresolved aspects of yourself that need to be brought into unity and wholeness. They will all be standing on the open area surrounding the pillar of light. Mentally direct these parts to line up and walk up the steps of the platform and into the light. As they walk into the pillar, they will be sucked inside the image of your core self. You may be surprised to see how many parts are milling about outside the light pillar—hundreds, possibly more.

Often when doing this you will find that some parts resist going into the pillar, and you may find demonic activity cropping up at times to prevent this process. You are dealing with sentient parts of yourself, so forcing them in will not work, but it is still useful and appropriate to pray against the demonic activity. Those parts that choose not to integrate at that time are simply not ready. Don't let it bother you if you there are many remaining—you just have more inner healing work to do in the future.

The Upgraded Fragment Plane

This method is similar to the first, but has some additional components. Instead of being on an inner plane inside yourself, take it to the throne room in heaven, placing your core self and the other parts in front of the Father who is seated there. See Jesus there with you, and scores of angels as well. A good way to start is by asking

Jesus to separate all the parts that are ready to integrate, then bring them in to merge with the core self. Your core self should still be inside a pillar of light, or if you prefer it can be a curtain made of the blood of Jesus that they have to pass through. Observe how Jesus and the angels work. Once all of the fragments that will join together are finished, ask the angels to minister to all of the parts who are close to being ready, but who aren't quite there yet. If you give them a few minutes to do this, you will find other parts who become ready to integrate. Finally, ask the angels to continue to work on the ones who aren't ready, and most especially for Jesus to reveal Himself to the fragments that don't know Him. This is a good time to exit the experience and let them continue working behind the scenes.

As mentioned before, this involves a certain style of inner healing modality that may not fit with everyone's background. That is perfectly fine. If there are elements of these two exercises that feel useful to you, such as appearing in the throne room and asking Jesus and the angels to minister to you, give them a try. Regardless of your beliefs on the matter, this is an opportunity to practice traveling in the spirit into the throne room of God; adapt it as you see fit.

Courtroom Practice

In Chapter 11 we discussed the Courts of Heaven. This is a prime opportunity to practice the principles shared there and to try out your own courtroom session. Remember that basic court work typically has four main parts: Accusation, Repentance, Forgiveness, and Ruling.

Take some time to go through these steps, starting with visualizing a heavenly courtroom. If this is your first time, ask Holy Spirit to help bring you into the scenario so you can get a good first experience. Then be Spirit-led as you go through the four steps to obtain your legal victory.

Out-of-Body Activation

Everyone wants to have out-of-body spirit travel experiences, and this is an advance version of the Correcting Your Vision exercise designed to help you do just that. As with the previous one, the goal is to do this while awake, body in a comfortable position. After you visualize stepping outside of your body, start going through your house. Where in the previous situation you were looking at yourself and your surroundings to correct your spiritual perception, the goal here is to explore. As you do so, consider what you see that might be occurring in real-time. Look out the window and watch cars drive by on the street. See what your pet animal is doing in another room. Go outside and observe the sky for clouds, planes, birds, or even just to see if you can see the position of the sun or moon correctly.

As you continue with this visualization and in-body spirit-travel practice, it is likely you will learn how to unlock the ability to go out-of-body during practice, and as you get better, to do so at will. While I understand this is not an accelerated means of engaging purposeful out-of-body travel, there are currently no wide-spread techniques for spirit travel by which this can be accomplished—something I expect to change as this revelation continues to grow and spread. As mentioned previously, the only ones that are out there are designed for astral projection, which I cannot guarantee will bring the desired results.

Partner Exercise

It is possible to practice spirit travel with a partner, and doing this is a good way to confirm and correct your spiritual vision as well. In this exercise, you will need to use a phone or walkie-talkie to speak to your partner, as you must move some distance away from one another. The nice thing is that you can even do this with a friend across the country—I have done this with someone in another state. The goal here is to practice perceiving the other person's surroundings and recounting them to him or her. You can look for things like colors and shapes or furniture, or try to see a design or drawing they have written on paper. When you receive confirmation that you have seen something accurately, try to hone in on what you are seeing to obtain more detail. The best way to do this is by taking turns sharing with one another what you see.

These are only some of the possible practice activities available, but they should help you either learn to spirit travel or enhance your current skill level. Remember that the only limit is your imagination, because God ". . . is able to do immeasurably more than all we ask or imagine, according to his power that is at work within us . . . (Ephesians 3:20). I would say the sky is the limit, but you can literally go anywhere in the heavens, cosmos, or the earth through spiritual travel. This is a means by which we can participate with God to combat forces of darkness, heal the sick and perform other forms of supernatural ministry, as well as obtain heavenly revelation. Traveling in the spirit is not the only tool in the tool belt, but it has a number of uses, and I hope this book has helped you to both understand its value and learn how to use it.

In conclusion, I would like to close with a prayer:

Heavenly Father, I thank you for the opportunity to delve deeper into your mysteries. I thank you for designing us from before the dawn of creation to be able to share in your Kingdom, and for allowing us to partner with You to extend that Kingdom. Thank you for your mercy and grace, and for your limitless kindness and love. We ask you to give us divine wisdom and guidance as we seek to learn and enhance our ability to travel in the spirit, and thank you for all of the assistance you bring us as we do this. We also ask for the angelic hosts to surround and protect us as we move forward, in Jesus name. Amen.

Other Books by

Michael C. King

Thank you for purchasing and reading *The Beginner's Guide to Traveling in the Spirit*. It is my sincere hope that this book has helped equip you to manifest the life of Jesus Christ in your life in a greater way. If you enjoyed it, you will find more free content at www.thekingsofeden.com. Please consider leaving a review on Amazon.com so others can find this book more easily.

Other books by Michael C. King include:
    Practical Keys to Raise the Dead
    The Gamer's Guide to the Kingdom of God
    Broken To Whole: Inner Healing for the Fragmented Soul

The Abundant Life Series
        Faith To Raise The Dead

The God Signs Series
        Gemstones From Heaven
        Feathers From Heaven

Appendix I

Spirit Travel "Target" Practice

1. Mona Lisa Painting
2. Big Ben Clock Tower
3. A bonfire
4. Napoleon Bonaparte
5. Library of Alexandria
6. A fork
7. Yellowstone Nat'l Park
8. A volcano
9. The Holy Grail
10. Mother Theresa

1. The Hope Diamond
2. Ark of the Covenant
3. Michael Jackson
4. Roses
5. Great Pyramids of Giza
6. Terra cotta soldiers
7. Edinburgh Castle
8. A hunting bow
9. Stonehenge
10. A slinky

1. Great Wall of China
2. Harriet Tubman
3. A canoe
4. The Sphinx
5. A wedding ring
6. North Pole
7. Last Supper Painting
8. A tomato
9. Albert Einstein
10. The Rosetta Stone

1. The Eiffel Tower
2. The Coliseum
3. A smartphone
4. Niagara Falls
5. A yo-yo
6. Noah's Ark
7. The Grand Canyon
8. Green grass
9. Nikola Tesla
10. A desert oasis

Excerpt from

Faith To Raise The Dead

Chapter 1: Back to Basics

When talking about raising the dead, one of the first things that comes to mind is an image of praying over a body. In actual practice it is daunting when standing there only to realize "I'm supposed to make him/her alive again? That's impossible!" Yes, technically it is, but God is in the business of doing the impossible, and when we start to think like God does, what was once unattainable starts to look extremely probable. This is why the resurrection process begins with one thing: Changing our thinking.

For centuries church members in all denominations have been taught many things about God that simply are not true, and in order to optimize success with raising the dead we need to revamp our understanding of God, take another look at what the *Bible* actually says about Him, and re-evaluate our long-held beliefs and what these things change for us. Then we will look at what we have actually been commanded to do. This means that we must go "back to basics" before heading on to the deeper stuff—which in reality isn't deep at all. The apostle Paul put it this way:

> In fact, though by this time you ought to be teachers, you need someone to teach you the elementary truths of God's word all over again. You need milk, not solid food! Anyone who lives on milk, being still an infant, is not acquainted with the teaching about righteousness. But solid food is for the mature, who by constant use have trained themselves to distinguish good from evil. Therefore let us move beyond the elementary teachings about Christ and be taken forward to maturity, not laying again the foundation of repentance from acts that lead to death, and of faith in God, instruction about cleansing rites, the laying on of hands, the *resurrection of the dead* [*emphasis mine*], and eternal judgment (Hebrews 5:12-6:2).

Resurrection is meant to be an elementary teaching of the faith, but more often than not it is shoved in a back corner somewhere, and I'm not entirely sure why. I have good friends who have had family members die and when I have politely offered to help pray for resurrection, they were resistant—to this day the deceased are still no longer with us. What I find so strange is that they are Charismatic and believe in resurrection, which usually means they would be open to it more than others of different denominations. It saddens me, actually, that what Jesus meant to be a basic part of the life of the believer has become this super-spiritual thing that special people do instead of what it is meant to be—part of a normal day in the life of a follower of Christ.

To truly understand God's will for resurrection, we need to grasp a few things first: God's original plan, His nature, and the purpose of healing. God's original plan was simple: Live forever. He didn't ever have to actually come out and say it because it was just that way.

We know this is true however because of what transpired in the Garden in Eden. If you need a refresher on the story reread Genesis Chapters 2 & 3.

In chapter 2, verses 16-17, "The Lord God commanded the man, 'You are free to eat from any tree in the garden; but you must not eat from the Tree of Knowledge of Good and Evil, for when you eat from it you will certainly die.'" Eating of the tree of the knowledge of good and evil caused death. Romans 5:12 says, "Therefore, just as sin entered the world through one man, and death through sin, and in this way death came to all people, because all sinned . . ." Once Adam and Eve ate from the forbidden tree, they lost their innate immortality and became mortal. Having unleashed death upon themselves and the rest of creation, Adam and Eve were powerless to fix it, so God intervened. The first thing He did was prevent the pair from eating from the Tree of Life again. Genesis 3: 22 states, "And the Lord God said, 'The man has now become like one of us, knowing good and evil. He must not be allowed to reach out his hand and take also from the tree of life and eat, and live forever.'" While this seems harsh, there is more to it than appears at first glance. We have been taught that because they didn't die immediately that what occurred was spiritual death, which did happen to a certain extent, but it is by no means the whole story and it is a doctrine that has thrown us off-track ever since. From the instant Adam and Eve ate the forbidden fruit their bodies began to decay. The life of God in that new world was so fresh that in spite of an imminent death sentence it took their bodies nearly a thousand years to wear out! How do we know God wasn't preventing them from living forever? We have to remember that Adam and Eve had free access to the Tree of Life prior to eating from the Tree of Knowledge of Good and Evil. They had *already* been immortal up to that time. God warned them that if they ate of the one tree that they would die—not because they would instantly drop dead, but because they lost their immunity to death and became subject to it. What God was doing was preventing their bodies from becoming immortal *in their fallen state.*

I once heard Kirby Delanerolle, cofounder of WOW Ministries in Sri Lanka, share a stunning revelation regarding this matter, explaining what God did in Genesis 3 to protect His children's access to the Tree of Life. Genesis 3:24 says, "After he drove the man out, he placed on the east side of the Garden of Eden cherubim and a flaming sword flashing back and forth to guard the way to the tree of life." God in His infinite kindness sent an angel with a flaming sword to guard the *way* to the Tree of Life. On the one hand it might seem like God was preventing Adam and Eve from taking the fruit, and in that moment He legitimately was in order to protect the couple, but the angel's job was not only to guard the tree, but the way to the tree. In other words, God was concerned about our access to life so He made sure that there is always an open road back—we will visit this again in the next chapter. That "guarded way" was brought to completion in Jesus Christ through His death and resurrection on the cross. The fact remains that God's will has always been for mankind to live an immortal and abundant life.

What does this mean for us? First, it puts the Garden events in a brand new light. God was acting as a kind and protective Father when He set up boundaries for His kids, not because He was angry with them but for their well-being. This could be compared to a fire in a fireplace. It heats the house in winter so we don't freeze, but we still have to keep our children from playing with it because we don't want them getting burned. Likewise, God knew that His kids were about to get hurt badly if He didn't act and prevent them from consuming the fruit of the Tree of Life in their fallen state. His solution was to stop the immediate danger and set an angelic guardian in place to temporarily restrict access while also protecting entry for the future.

If we accept that God's original plan was for man to never die, it stands to reason that God isn't a big fan of death. And really, He isn't—death is God's enemy, in total opposition to His life-giving nature. In spite of this, the Church has taught us that God kills people. Well, we don't like to put it in such harsh and uncultured language, preferring the more delicate version of "God takes people home" but we can't honestly have God "taking people home" without Him killing them. Either God kills people to get them to heaven or death is an enemy and God doesn't kill, but we can't have it both ways. We will look at this a bit more in a future chapter, but let me throw out a verse for you to chew on until later. First Corinthians 12:25-26 says, "For he [Jesus] must reign until he has put all his enemies under his feet. The last enemy to be destroyed is death." Death is an enemy—God's enemy, and therefore ours as well.

If God values life immensely and He never meant for mankind to die, it only stands to reason that He would make a provision for resurrection. In fact, it's hard for God *not* to value life because it's His very nature. John 1:1-4 says, "In the beginning was the Word, and the Word was with God, and the Word was God. He was with God in the beginning. Through him all things were made; without him nothing was made that has been made. In him was life, and that life was the light of all mankind." Jesus and God are one and the same so this passage shows that God's nature—the very essence of His being, is made of life. It is impossible for God to want anything *other* than life for us because to do so would be against His nature. Jesus expressed yet again in John 10:10 how much he values life saying, "The thief comes only to steal and kill and destroy; I have come that they may have life, and have it to the full." Full, abundant life is what Jesus is after for all of us, and he stopped at nothing short of *His* death to wrest the power of death from the enemy, thereby giving us the authority to command the dead to rise again.

Works Cited

Amos, Jonathan. "'Quadruple helix' DNA seen in human cells." *BBC News*. BBC, 20 Jan. 2013. Web. 6 Apr. 2017. <http://www.bbc.com/news/science-environment-21091066>.

Cox, Paul. "Aslans Place." *Aslans Place*. N.p., 26 June 2013. Web. 4 May 2017. <http://aslansplace.com/language/en/yada-and-the-gift-of-discernment-paul-l-cox/>.

Doyle, Arthur Conan, and Sidney Paget. *A Scandal in Bohemia*. Chelmsford, England: Goode Press, 2005. Print.

Hope. Personal Interview. 12 June 2017

"Padre Pio: Bilocation and Odor of Sanctity." Padre Pio The Mystic -Bilocation. N.p., n.d. Web. 13 May 2017. <https://www.ewtn.com/padrepio/mystic/bilocation.htm>.

Strong, James. Strong's Exhaustive Concordance. Peabody, MA: Hendrickson, 2007. Blueletterbible.com. Web. 5 Oct. 2016.

Tan, Peter. The Spiritual World. Peter Tan Evangelism: Canberra, AU 2007. PDF.

Thayer, Joseph H. The New Thayer's Greek-English Lexicon of the New Testament. Peabody, MA: Hendrickson, 1981.

About the Author

Michael King is a prolific writer by day and a Registered Nurse by night. He hungrily explores all things spiritual and his love for God has given him a passion for signs, wonders, and miracles. Michael is married to a beautiful wife who doubles as his professional editor. He is known by family and friends for his proficiency in the prophetic and in healing prayer and energy work. His blog, thekingsofeden.com, focuses on spirituality with a hint of health-related topics along with a dash of his fiction and fantasy writing. He is available for speaking engagements on request.

www.ingramcontent.com/pod-product-compliance
Lightning Source LLC
LaVergne TN
LVHW011326080426
835513LV00006B/216